The Political Economy
of Growth

To Barbara, Jackie, Donald and Fergus

DAVID SIMPSON

The Political Economy
of Growth

Classical Political Economy and the Modern World

St. Martins Press · New York

ISBN 0-312-62232-5

Library of Congress Cataloging in Publication Data

Simpson, David.
    The political economy of growth.

    1. Economic development.   2. Economic history –
1971–   3. Economic Policy.   I. Title.
HD82.S5555   1983   338.9   82-23168
ISBN 0-312-62232-5

Contents

Preface

It has been suggested that the annual revisions to the official National Accounts prepared by the Central Statistical Offices of each country cease, not because an acceptable degree of accuracy in the estimates has been achieved, but because the services of the statisticians thus employed are required for other, more pressing, tasks. In much the same way, this book, which has been through innumerable drafts and has been some ten years in the making, has finally been published.

Although the book has many remaining defects, I am aware that I owe a particular apology to students of classical political economy for my cavalier treatment of their subject. The justification for allowing the contents of the following chapters to be published is that I believe that the theme of the book is an important one, however inadequately it is expressed.

This theme is that, if we wish to understand the operation of a modern advanced economy, we must escape from many of the 'habitual modes of thought and expression' associated with contemporary neo-classical and neo-Keynesian economic theory, and adopt the long-run perspective of classical political economy, concerning in particular such phenomena as the nature of competition and growth in a market economy, and the evolution of institutions and attitudes. In the recent past, a small but growing number of books has been written in this tradition (I should like to believe that it is not an accident that a disproportionate number of these have come from the Scottish universities), but very few departments have offered courses in political economy. It is therefore encouraging to discover, at the time of writing, that such courses are slowly beginning to return to the curriculum, albeit at the post-graduate level.

I am grateful for comments and criticisms of various sections of earlier drafts to Paul Hare, Frank Harrigan, Jim McGilvray and Iain McNicoll. I am profoundly indebted to Professor Peter Bauer, whose advice and criticism encouraged me to complete the manuscript. My colleagues at the Fraser of Allander Institute have borne additional burdens of work while this book was being written, and the secretaries at the Institute, Mrs Sheelagh Blackhall, Mrs Isobel Sheppard and Miss Patricia Cassells have, with great patience, typed and re-typed the various drafts. The index has been compiled by my wife, Barbara Simpson.

David Simpson
The Fraser of Allander Institute
University of Strathclyde

Economic analysis, serving for two centuries to win an under-standing of the Nature and Causes of the Wealth of Nations has been fobbed off with another bride, a Theory of Value ... Faced with the choice . . . economists of the last hundred years have sacrificed dynamic theory in order to discuss relative prices. This has been unfortunate, first because an assumption of static overall conditions is such a drastic departure from reality as to make it impossible to submit anything evolved within it to the test of verification and, secondly, because it ruled out the discussion of most of the problems that are actually interesting and condemned econ-omics to the arid formalism satirised by J. H. Clapham in 'Of Empty Economic Boxes'.

Joan Robinson, *The Accumulation of Capital,*
London, 1966, p.v

1

Introduction

This book is concerned with the scope and method of contemporary economic analysis. Its starting-points are the major problems of economic policy common to the advanced industrialized countries of the Western world. Many of these problems are shared by the developing countries and by the countries of Eastern Europe, but it is on the experience of those countries which for practical purposes can be identified as member countries of the Organization for Economic Co-operation and Development (OECD) that I wish to draw for empirical evidence.

The book tries to demonstrate that the major problems currently besetting these advanced economies can best be understood within the framework of a theory of economic growth. This is so because the advanced economies of the modern world are characterized primarily by continuous change. Unfortunately, contemporary economic analysis, whether neo-classical or neo-Keynesian, does not provide a satisfactory theory of economic growth, and therefore we must turn to the classical tradition, with its much richer and broader scope, for the necessary ingredients. Nothing as ambitious as a comprehensive theory of growth will be offered; like Schumpeter, I do not aspire to do more than to identify tendencies. But I do believe that an approach to a theory of economic growth in the classical tradition can contribute more to an understanding of the way advanced economies actually behave than can be found in the 'arid formalism' of steady-state growth theories.

It is curious that, although Adam Smith made institutions the key instrument variables (as we should now say) of his famous theory of growth, and although experiments in institutional reform as an aid to growth are a feature of the contemporary scene in Eastern Europe and in some developing countries, the role of institutional change has for long been disregarded in economic theorizing in the Western world. This may be because we have come to believe that institutional arrangements in the advanced countries have reached a state of ultimate perfection (as both Smith and, later, Marx believed their own schemes represented). It is more likely that institutions and other 'non-economic' variables have been forgotten because the theory of economic growth has gradually been replaced by the theory of value as the principal subject of interest to economists in the advanced countries. Closely related to this phenomenon is the terminological dichotomy whereby there is supposed to be a separate and distinct theory of growth for developing countries, called the 'theory of economic development', as if the growth process in developing and advanced countries was somehow different.[1]

Because of its connotation of having a broader range of variables within its scope, this book might appropriately have contained the words 'economic development' within its title. However, this phrase has become so closely associated with the underdeveloped countries that it was considered preferable to avoid it. The term 'political economy', too, has been so abused by contemporary writers that it is only with the greatest reluctance that it is used here.[2] The use of that term in this book is intended to convey its original sense, that is, the study of economics in the classical tradition, which has three principal characteristics that distinguish it from contemporary analysis. First, it takes the long-term growth and development of the economic system as its principal object of study; secondly, it recognizes that social, psychological and other non-economic variables must therefore explicitly be taken into account; and thirdly, it has a much wider range of methods of analysis which are admissible than is the practice in contemporary analysis.

The main chapters of the book can conveniently be grouped into three parts. The first three chapters discuss the failure of contemporary economic analysis to deal satisfactorily with the issues of economic policy in the advanced countries. This factor is attributed primarily to the lack of an adequate theory of economic growth. Chapters 4 and 5 set out the classical tradition in the analysis of economic growth, and identify those elements which may be helpful in contributing to a contemporary theory. The purpose of chapter 4 is to establish similarities between the contributions of different writers in the classical tradition, and thereby provide a framework for the analysis of economic growth which may be helpful in understanding contemporary problems. This chapter concentrates on the general features of the major writers and, in particular, on the role which they assigned to institutions and attitudes as variables in the process of growth. The word 'attitudes' is used loosely to include all psychological variables, such as motives and expectations. Chapter 5 discusses two central themes of the classical theory of growth – the nature of competition and the progressive extension of the division of labour.

Chapter 6 discusses some important changes in the advanced economies which have taken place in the recent past, within the perspective developed in chapters 4 and 5. Chapter 7 analyses the origins of some contemporary problems in the economies of the advanced countries. Chapter 8 outlines some probable future developments: what is most likely to happen. The concluding chapter, chapter 10, considers, on the other hand, what might be done on the part of governments to influence the outcome of events. Between these two chapters comes chapter 9, which proposes some changes of emphasis in the methods of contemporary economic analysis.

Much economic theorizing in the period following the Second World War, especially on the subject of economic growth, has taken the form of the presentation of essentially simple ideas in extremely sophisticated or difficult terms. This would appear to be a continued pursuit of the 'arid formalism' criticized by Clapham after the First World War.

One purpose of this book is to return to the classical tradition of presenting somewhat more sophisticated ideas in relatively simple terms. Although nothing is easier than making fun of the shortcomings of contemporary economics, the intention is to put forward a positive alternative.

Another theme of the book is the desirability of reintegrating economics with the other social sciences. Although I agree with Marshall that one single theory of social science is probably impossible, it is suggested here that what is essential is the recognition that 'economic' events seldom have an exclusively economic character, but more often than not are multidimensional. In this connection it is appropriate to quote from John Stuart Mill:

> Except on matters of detail there are perhaps no practical questions, even among those which approach nearest to the character of purely economic questions, which admit to being decided on economic premises alone. And it is because Adam Smith never loses sight of this truth, because in his applications of political economy he perpetually appeals to other and often far larger considerations than pure political economy affords, he gives that well-grounded feeling of command over the principles of the subject for purposes of practice, owing to which the Wealth of Nations, alone among treatises of political economy, has not only been popular with general readers, but has impressed itself strongly on the minds of men of the world and of legislators.[3]

2

Objectives of Economic Policy in the Advanced Countries

For present purposes the advanced countries may be taken as being congruent with the member countries of OECD.[1] Despite their differences, these countries share a number of common problems. Indeed, it is probably true to say that, as time goes by, the commonness of their problems increases, so that, although there may or may not be convergence between 'capitalist' and 'socialist' countries, there is certainly convergence among the advanced countries themselves.

I shall begin by identifying six problems which represent contemporary policy preoccupations in these countries. It is not suggested that all of the advanced countries manifest all of these problems, but that most of the seven major industrialized countries (the United States, Japan, West Germany, France, the United Kingdom, Italy and Canada), which account for by far the greater part of economic activity in the advanced countries as a whole, do exhibit most of them. These problems are:

1 inflation;
2 unemployment;
3 slow rates of growth of total output and productivity;
4 the environmental consequences of the growth of output;
5 the psychological consequences of the growth of output;
6 the nature and limits of government control of economic activity.

This list may be regarded as incomplete. I have left out the underdeveloped countries as a problem, since I do not believe that, as a group, these countries have a decisive influence on events in the advanced countries. This is not to say that particular underdeveloped countries at particular periods of time do not have such an influence.

Although I will discuss in later chapters the inequality of incomes within countries, I have not identified income distribution as one of the stylized problems, principally because it does not appear to be a major preoccupation of policy in North America or Japan, and its importance as an issue varies throughout Western Europe.

The balance of payments has been omitted on the grounds that, where it is a problem for a particular advanced country, it is usually not a separate problem but simply another symptom of one of the first three problems listed above. Of course, these three may not be regarded as independent problems, but rather as separate symptoms of a common underlying problem. This is the view which is taken in this book. These symptoms have been related to each other by the popular press and given the phrase 'the English disease', first observed some two decades ago and more recently observed to have spread to the USA, Sweden and even to West Germany. The symptoms of the disease are a poor performance in all three areas, sustained over a period of more than five years.

It must be said right away that the concept of a 'poor' performance is not necessarily to be judged by comparison with the past performance of the country concerned. Nor is the relevant comparison with the performance of other advanced countries, though both types of comparison are made, and are often influential. Rather, performance is judged by reference to the expectations of the country's inhabitants. Thus a 'problem' arises from a discrepancy between an expected or assumed norm and reality. It may be the case that the cause of the problem is the selection of an inappropriate norm.

Unlike the first three items, the fourth and fifth problems are associated with the consequences rather than with the causes of growth of output, and with faster growth rather than slower growth. Economists who have recently drawn attention to the adverse psychological consequences of sustained growth of output include Hirsch and Scitovsky; those associated with concern for the environment include Forrester, Meadows and Schumacher; while Mishan and Heilbroner are concerned with both. The distinction drawn between the physical and psychological consequences of growth may be blurred. It is not clear, for example, whether tourist 'pollution' should be regarded as a physical or a psychological problem.

The final item may not appear to be so much an object of policy as an instrument of policy. Nevertheless, it is easy to see that the discontents generated by contemporary industrialized life do give rise to political demands, or perhaps give added strength to existing political demands. Although this item may not appear to affect directly the performance of the economy, the appropriate nature and limits of government control in the advanced economy does concern the choice of instruments by which performance is influenced. It also concerns the political institutions of the country. I have included this as a 'problem' because it does seem to be both a matter of continuing debate and of continuing change in practice in the advanced countries. It is clearly related to all of the other items.

It is my contention that the origins and nature of these six problems can best be understood within one framework of analysis, which it is the principal object of this book to present. I do not claim that the proposed framework of analysis will resolve these problems. I deprecate the rush into policy recommendations on the basis of an inadequate understanding of the economic process which is the hallmark of so much of contemporary economics. I do, however, think that policies which are developed in the light of this framework may have a greater chance of success than those which are not. First, however, I shall say a little more about each of the problems identified.

Inflation

In contrast to the period between the two world wars when prices were either stable (1920s) or fell (1930s), there has been a continuous and accelerating rise in prices in the advanced countries since the Second World War. The rate of increase of prices averaged 3 per cent in the 1950s, 4 per cent in the 1960s and 8 per cent in the 1970s. However, the upward drift has not been a steady one. An examination of the inflation rates for the seven major industrialized economies, and for OECD as a whole, shows that until the year 1967 the average annual price increases shown by both series never reached 4 per cent. But from 1968, the average increase never fell below 4 per cent, and from 1973 never below 7 per cent. The other major discontinuity displayed by these two series is the acceleration into double figures in the years 1974 and 1975 following the first round of oil price increases.[2] The same two series returned to double figures in 1980 and 1981, following the second round of major oil price increases.

An increase in the rate of inflation has not been the only response of the advanced economies to the oil price increases. As we shall see below, the reactions within the advanced economies to these exogenous 'shocks' provide case studies in the individual adaptability of each economy to change. However, inflation is important for a number of reasons, not least that it has widely been held to be subversive of existing institutions and attitudes. In Schumpeter's words, it 'quickens the pace of social change'. Perhaps for this reason, inflation appears to be regarded as a greater evil than unemployment by inhabitants of the advanced countries. This is suggested by the fact that the second round of oil price increases evoked a uniform response from the governments of the major industrialized countries. All adopted and have maintained tight monetary and fiscal policies. The absence of strong popular opposition to these policies hitherto suggests that the preference of the governments may be shared by the populace as a whole.[3]

The effect of inflation on political institutions and attitudes may be intangible and delayed: the effects on economic institutions are more directly perceived and more immediate.[4] In view of these official policy responses, popular attitudes and damaging consequences, one is bound to ask why the great acceleration of inflation in the 1970s was tolerated by the governments of the advanced countries? Was the failure one of technique or of understanding of the process itself? Or were the governments of the advanced countries powerless to arrest the inflation? If so, this must cast doubt on their ability to achieve their objectives in other areas of economic policy, and to raise again the question why this should be so. In fairness, it must be said that the rate of increase in prices after the second round of oil price increases was very much less than that which took place after the first round.

Unemployment

Although measures of unemployment differ amongst many of the advanced countries, and there are problems of disguised unemployment in both public and private sectors, there is unmistakable statistical evidence of upward movements in the levels of measured unemployment in each of the advanced countries since the Second World War. In the early post-war period, unemployment as a percentage of the labour force was at first very low. According to Maddison, it averaged only 2.9 per cent in Western Europe for the 1950s and 1.5 per cent for the 1960s, compared with 3.3 per cent for the 1920s and 7.5 per cent for the 1930s.[5] The 1970s, however, exhibited a very different picture. For the first half of the decade, unemployment rates for the seven major economies, and for the industrialized countries as a whole, averaged between 3 per cent and 4 per cent, whereas in the second half the rates averaged over 5 per cent. In 1981, the rate has moved to over 6 per cent for both series, and shows little prospect of falling to the level which prevailed until 1974.

Even more remarkable than the change in statistics has been the change in public policy manifested within the last decade. For thirty years after 1945 the conventional belief in the Western world was that unemployment could always be relieved by the government acting to increase aggregate demand. It now appears to be believed by most policy-makers, and most − if not all − academic economists, not only that such action may have harmful side-effects, such as accelerating the rate of inflation, but that it may not even increase the level of employment in the long run. This view was stated publicly by the then British Prime Minister, Mr James Callaghan, at the 1976 Labour Party Conference, when he said, 'we cannot spend our way out of a recession'.[6] This view has been endorsed in practice by the other major advanced countries, since none have adopted 'Keynesian' policies in response to the rising unemployment of 1980 and 1981.

Slow growth of output and productivity

According to Maddison, 'in Western Europe the average growth of output in the 1950s was 4.4% per year, which was substantially better than the 1920s. The decade of the 1960s was even better with an average growth rate of 5.2%. The 1960s performance was more homogeneous than that of the 1950s. The period 1950−70 was remarkably free of cyclical disturbance. There was an absence of serious business fluctuations with virtually no loss of output because of the recession.' Once again, the series shows a marked change in behaviour in the 1970s. Up to 1973 the growth rate of the 1960s was maintained by the industrialized countries. Following the recession and recovery of the years 1974−76, neither the seven major economies nor the industrialized countries as a whole have been able to return to their previous annual average rates of growth. Even the Japanese growth rate, which had been 8 per cent per annum, has come down to 3−4 per cent. 1975 was the first year since the war when the advanced countries as a whole experienced an absolute fall in output. It may be significant for our purposes that, whereas growth rates in the 1960s appear in retrospect to have been satisfactory, dissatisfaction with 'slow' rates of growth appear to have been greatest in that same decade, to judge by the tenor of public debate and informed opinion at the time.

Adverse environmental effects

Although the environmental effects of economic activity are less well documented than many other aspects of economic life, and although the nature and extent of these effects have been keenly debated in recent years, two propositions may confidently be advanced. First, that there have been adverse environmental effects and, secondly, that they flow from what E. J. Mishan has called 'the collective pursuit of economic growth' in the advanced countries. Amongst the effects cited by that writer are the pollution of land, sea and air, the 'uglification' of cities the world over, the sacrifice of areas of natural beauty to the tourist trade, the depletion of non-renewable resources and the accumulation of hazardous and indestructible materials.[7]

The significance of these effects for the purposes of this book are as follows. First, there is an increasing discrepancy between measured aggregate output and welfare, as illustrated by Mishan's observation that:

> Official exhortations to faster economic growth are so often rationalised by reference to the immense resources needed to deal with mounting social and environmental problems that are themselves the chief legacy of rapid economic growth.[8]

Secondly, an extension of government intervention in the market economy is called for. Not only do pollution and uglification require resources for their abatement; to the extent that they are not eliminated, they impose external disutilities on individual consumers. This justifies government intervention in the price system on grounds of allocative efficiency. At the same time, the accumulation of hazardous materials, another by-product of collective growth, calls for government intervention on grounds of security. However, even in advanced countries, government intervention is not an institutional arrangement which is characterized by its flexibility or smoothness of adjustment. Indeed, it is frequently the result of political pressures from particular interest groups which use the institutions of government, legislative or otherwise, to resist socially desirable adjustments. Although the physical exhaustion of many non-renewable resources is most likely in the foreseeable future, the price changes which would make this less likely are often limited by government action.

Adverse psychological effects

Explicit in the neo-classical theory of value and implicit in Marx is the notion that utility or satisfaction is an increasing function of the level of consumption of material goods. There can certainly be no doubt that the advanced countries have experienced rising levels of material consumption for at least the past century Accordingly, one should expect to find a continuing rise in the level of satisfaction of the inhabitants of these countries. But in the post-war period, just when the rise in material consumption has been most rapid, it has been observed that there has been a sustained upward movement in such indicators as divorce, suicide, delinquency, petty theft, drug-taking, alcoholism, sexual deviation and violence. These are symptoms of what Mishan calls 'social disintegration' and what Schumacher calls 'the loss of cultural integrity'. It should be noted that it has only been asserted, and not demonstrated, that these indicators are linked with continuing economic growth. It is possible that there are other causes, such as a sense of vulnerability to extermination by nuclear weapons. Associated with this movement, some commentators see a general erosion of standards of taste and propriety in the advanced countries, and others detect an increasing emotional enfeeblement amongst their inhabitants.

A number of explanations have been put forward to establish a connection between rising consumption and apparently declining satisfaction. There is, first of all, the explanation in terms of the effects of the accelerating rate of technological change upon the individual's sense of security and desire for familiarity. There is then the suggestion that consumer satisfaction in advanced economies comes from relative and not from absolute consumption levels; the implication of this is that a neighbour's acquisition of material goods excites envy and dissatisfaction. Then there is the anti-materialist view that:

> Once subsistence levels are exceeded, the possession of more goods is neither the sole nor the chief source of men's satisfaction; indeed the technical means designed to pursue further material ends may produce a civilisation uncongenial to the psychic needs of ordinary men. A civilisation offering increasing opportunities for rapid movement, titillation, research, effortless living and push-button entertainment does not compensate for a deepening sense of something lost: of the myths, perhaps, on which men's self-esteem depends; of a sense of belonging; of the easy flow of sympathy and feeling between members of a group; of the enduring loyalty that comes only from hardships borne together; of a sense of space and un-pre-empted leisure and of the solidity of the here and now.[9]

This passage contains two essential ideas. The first, which can be traced back as far as Adam Smith, and in our time has been repeated by Weil and Hirsch among others, is that the positive relationship between material consumption and satisfaction breaks down once a certain level of consumption has been attained. Just how far beyond subsistence that level lies has never been defined, but the idea is clear. It is the distinction between needs and wants. If this is an explanation for the association between rising material consumption and increasing discontent, then it has to be reconciled with the other observation that the drive for improvement in the individual household's own material living standards shows few signs of abating in the advanced countries. This is so if one judges by the results of the electoral process in the United Kingdom and the United States, where the primary factor determining the popularity of a government still appears to be the performance of the country's economy during that government's period of office, for which it is — rightly or wrongly — held to be responsible. The reconciliation can be achieved, if it is assumed either (a) that people do not know what gives them satisfaction, or (b) that the majority of people in the advanced countries have still not reached that level of material consumption where the possession of more goods is no longer their chief source of satisfaction.

The second essential idea contained in the passage quoted above is that the economic institutions and technology required to raise material living standards for large numbers of people have direct psychological effects which are adverse in terms of satisfaction, and more than offset the potential gains in satisfaction which are produced by the increased material consumption. In other words, although *one* person alone would gain from a rise in his material living standards, both for the Hirsch reasons and because there would be no adverse psychological effects, a quite different set of institutions, attitudes and technology is required in order to produce the level of output necessary for an increase in material living standards for everyone.

A third point, not touched upon in the passage quoted, but closely related, is that once material living standards have risen to a certain level, then the traditional values such as self-sacrifice, hard work, parsimony, frugality, etc., associated with earlier stages of economic growth, become redundant. From the standpoint of the economy this may be quite acceptable, but from two other standpoints it may be less so. From a political standpoint, there is reason to believe that a democratic system cannot function if each group within that society pushes to the limit its 'rights', that is, acts self-indulgently rather than with self-restraint. From a moral standpoint, these traditional values not only supported the process of economic growth and are explicit in the recipe for growth set out in *The Wealth of Nations*, but they are among the essential values of Christianity and of Western civilization as a whole.

Government control of the economy

Whether one goes back for a century or more or only as far as the Second World War, there can be little doubt that government involvement has increased in all the advanced economies.[10] Heilbroner identifies four phases of growth in the extent of government intervention in the US economy. From the earliest times to the mid-nineteenth century, there were government subsidies to or direct investments in such infrastructure as roads, canals and schools. From the mid-nineteenth century to the 1930s, there was a proliferation of government regulatory agencies. From the late 1930s to the 1960s, there was a period of active monetary and fiscal policies designed to achieve politically desired levels of employment, growth and welfare. Since the 1970s, the question of wage and price controls has come to be a policy issue. Although the timing and nature of government intervention has differed from one country to another, the trend is unmistakable and the pattern is one of convergence. In the United States and the United Kingdom the tendencies which Schumpeter identified as marking a transition from capitalism to socialism have continued much as he predicted.[11] In the context of the contemporary advanced countries in general, the rather academic question of the appropriate limits of government control of the economy has resolved itself into three practical issues. First, there is the issue of the efficient allocation of resources: not only the degree of public-sector monopolies, but the distribution of resources within and between the public sector and the rest of the economy. This is connected with the problem of slow growth. Secondly, the implication for political freedom of the growth of corporations (the influence of trade unions, major corporations and state power). Finally there is the critical issue of what Schumpeter called 'the socialisation of the labour market', that is, the imposition by government of wages and price controls upon the economy. Hitherto such controls have only been temporary, and have been forced by the logic of events on supposedly unwilling governments. The crucial question is whether permanent statutory wage and price controls are likely to be avoided and, if so, by what means.

3

The Failure of Contemporary Economic Analysis

This chapter begins with evidence that contemporary economic analysis[1] has failed to contribute significantly to an understanding of the more important economic policy problems in the advanced countries of the present day. The possibility that a lack of data is at fault is considered and rejected. It is then argued that an excessive preoccupation with quantitative methods has led to attention being confined to a limited class of relationships – those which are easily quantifiable. It is not argued that quantitative methods in economics are wrong, but that they are inappropriate when applied to the kinds of problems to which economic policy in the advanced countries has largely been directed. In the following section it is argued that the scope of contemporary analysis is limited to an excessively narrowly defined set of variables, excluding such things as institutions and attitudes. Finally, it is argued that current problems in the advanced countries require for their proper understanding a theory of economic growth, and that the failure of contemporary analysis to provide this is due chiefly to the fact that it does not possess a theory of economic growth at all.

Brief review of contemporary economic analysis

Over the past twenty years or more the state of the art and science of economics has received periodic appraisal from some of its more distinguished practitioners. All have agreed that in the post-war period economic theory has been refined to a degree of sophistication and intellectual difficulty previously undreamed of. All but one are agreed that this progress in theory has not been matched by progress in results.[2]

The critics begin by acknowledging the refinement of the structure of economic theory. Phelps Brown suggests that the most important developments of economic theory in the past thirty years have included the refinement of the logic of resource allocation, the building of growth models and the econometric analysis of national economic systems. But Koopmans concludes: 'we must face the fact that models using elaborate theoretical and statistical tools and concepts have not done decisively better, in the majority of available tests, than the most simpleminded mechanical extrapolation formulae'. Lowe, on the same theme, writes: 'to put it bluntly, our ability to explain and to predict has not improved in proportion to the exactitude of the method applied'.

Leontief also expresses doubts about the true worth of the refinement of theory. He refers to 'the slight substantive content of the argument behind the formidable front of algebraic signs', and concludes: 'in no other field of empirical enquiry has so massive and sophisticated a statistical machinery been used with such indifferent results'. Thus, these leading academic practitioners conclude that the developments in economic theory since the Second World War have failed to produce results in the form of an improved understanding of the economic issues of our time.

If we look at the evidence offered by economists who practise in government or in business, the conclusions are equally negative. O'Brien reports that business economists discover that 'very little of what they learned in university turned out to explain anything at all'. Phelps Brown is even more blunt: he points out that training in advanced economics has been reported to be 'actively unhelpful' in making government or business decisions. This disappointing finding should be compared with the optimistic claim made fifteen years earlier that those trained in the new economics 'have been in great demand in industry and in government service . . . because their analytical training is found to be directly relevant to the making of business or government decisions about future policy'.[3]

Applied economic forecasting in the post-war period has been noted for its failures rather than its successes. A representative example is the semi-annual forecasts of the performance of the advanced economies prepared by the OECD. An analysis of the outcome of these forecasts showed that they performed little better than naive forecasts.[4]

A fourth category of failure can be identified in the singular lack of success which distinguished economists have had when acting as senior policy advisers to the government. To their credit, some have admitted in published articles the limitations of their role. Others have been more reticent, but none have claimed success. One cannot help thinking of the contrast between the analytical sophistication of the adviser and the performance of the corresponding economy in the case of Oskar Lange and the Polish economy, W. A. Lewis and the Ghanaian economy, and the expertise − both internal and external − at the disposal of the UK Treasury in relation to the actual performance of the UK economy in the 1960s and the 1970s.

It is a distinguished British economist, however, who remains confident that nothing much is wrong with contemporary economic analysis. Concluding his presidential address to the Royal Economic Society on 24 July 1980, Sir Richard Stone said 'the world may be going to the dogs, but economics certainly is not'.[5] Stone did not, however, address himself to the arguments put forward by the others. His argument is threefold. First, there have been substantial technical improvements: 'the gaps between the *a priori* and the empirical have narrowed considerably', and 'tools on offer to the policymaker are getting more and more sophisticated'. As we have seen, this would not be denied by the critics. More questionable is his claim that 'society has in some measure benefited from the progress of economic science: the prosperity of the

1950s and the 1960s was partly brought about by the application of a number of prescriptions recommended in the 1920s and the 1930s if not earlier'. Although it would be generally agreed that the economic performance of the UK in the 1960s was superior to that in the 1930s, it is not immediately obvious that the performance in the 1970s was better than that in the 1920s. Furthermore, confidence in the efficacy of Keynesian prescriptions waned amongst economists of all persuasions during the 1970s, and had vanished almost completely by the end of the decade. This was not due so much to certain problems of interpretation, as to the prolonged coexistence of inflation and unemployment in most of the advanced countries. Very few economists today believe that the growth rates of the 1950s and 1960s, which appear in retrospect so satisfactory, were simply the result of clever management of aggregate demand.

Apart from the defence on technical grounds, and on the more doubtful grounds of improved performance, Stone's third argument seems to be that people expect too much of government. He continues: 'prosperity is threatened, partly because the correct doses have been exceeded, partly because the physicians have been oblivious of side effects, and partly because new diseases have manifested themselves'. It is with the third part of this statement that critics would most strongly disagree. It will be argued in this book that the diagnosis has been wrong, and that the observed diseases are not new but only symptoms of old and deep-seated diseases, which are endemic to the patient's condition. Specifically, it will be argued that the sustained growth of the advanced economies in the recent past has produced changes in institutions and in attitudes within these societies which are responsible for our present 'diseases'. These 'diseases' do not come from outside the economic process, but are produced by the process itself.

To summarize then, the majority of leading practitioners who have reviewed the state of economics are agreed that contemporary economic analysis has had disappointing results. Attempts at forecasting on the basis of this analysis have been unsuccessful, and training in this analysis has been unhelpful in decision-making, whether in business or in government.

Lack of data

All of these reviewers have gone on to advance reasons for this failure. Leontief writes: 'the uneasiness of which I spoke is caused not by the irrelevance of the practical problems to which present day economists address their efforts, but rather by the palpable inadequacy of the scientific means by which they try to solve them' The same writer makes it clear that, in his view, the primary reason for this inadequacy is the lack of data, and this is a view which is widely held by quantitative economists. So far as quantitative methods are concerned, it cannot be denied that the development of ever more sophisticated statistical techniques and of ever more intricate mathematical reasoning cannot make up for the weakness of the data base.

The great difficulty with the availability of primary data is that 'in contrast to most physical sciences we study a system that is not only exceedingly complex but is also in a state of constant flux'. Koopmans argues that, as a consequence of the lack of data, 'we do not know which basic assumptions about the behaviour of the strategic decision-making units are empirically relevant. Until we do, model building will be a branch of mathematics and logic, rather than a powerful tool for an empirical science.'

On the same point, Phelps Brown comments that Marshall's confidence that economists could, for example, predict the ways in which 'fluctuations of credit will affect foreign trade' was based on there being 'dependable propensities of economic behaviour, apparent to the observer of everyday affairs'. But Phelps Brown asserts that such dependable propensities no longer exist. He asks rhetorically: 'what effects do changes in rates of interest have on business decisions? How do managers react to different forms of investment incentive?' We might also add, how do consumers react to the rise or fall in the rate of inflation, in terms of their savings? If the 'dependable propensities' to which Marshall refers did really once exist but no longer do exist, then this supports the argument of Lowe that there are no longer sufficient empirical regularities to justify an economic theory of the behaviour of advanced economic systems. It is Lowe's opinion that the government should therefore intervene to restore regularity to the macro-economic processes.

In my own opinion, there are indeed regularities to be perceived in the existing processes of advanced economies, but they are not those that can easily or usefully be quantified. Nor do they correspond to those parameters which occur in steady-state growth theory, neo-classical value theory or neo-Keynesian theories of the trade cycle. Such parameters tend to be either unstable or of little help in understanding the nature of the process of growth in advanced economies.

Harmful influence of quantitative methods

The application of quantitative methods of analysis to economics is not new: it can be traced at least as far back as John Stuart Mill. Indeed it has been claimed that as early as the middle of the nineteenth century economics 'had purged itself of all the philosophical, political and sociological residues of its origin'.[6] As a consequence, the huge body of knowledge incorporating these matters has not been passed on to the next generation of economists. In order that this knowledge should be restored to succeeding generations, it will be necessary to expand the teaching of the history of economic thought in universities.

The tide of positivism carried quantitative methods to a new high-water mark of influence in economics in the early 1960s. Indeed, it has come to occupy the dominating position in economics. This has had a number of harmful consequences. It has become part of the practice of quantitative analysis for it to omit the historical context from which its data are drawn. In this way, a potentially rich source of information is thrown away. In statistical time-series analysis, it is forgotten that each country, each firm and each household has its own particular characteristics.

Secondly, the application of quantitative methods in economics has seemed to overlook the fact that the agents in the economic process differ fundamentally from the basic units observed in most of the natural sciences. They react purposefully and spontaneously, both as individuals and as collective groups. Thus the economic process cannot be represented as the interaction of robotic units without excluding the social as well as the individual nature of the process. This point has been frequently made both by Marxists and Austrians. Not only individuals, but groups are able to learn from past experience. Thus, it has been suggested[7] that in the United Kingdom the growing awareness of the supposed existence of the Phillips curve helped to remove whatever tenuous validity it ever had. In general, if the future pattern of economic behaviour differs from the past, in part because of changes in collective or individual decisions arising from experience of the past, then one may question the usefulness of empirical data (which must, by definition, relate to the past), except as an exercise in economic history. For example, if in year t a society votes to have an incomes policy, and in year $t + 2$ to have a different kind of such policy, of what value can observations be which pertain to behaviour in year $t - 1$? If people continuously adapt their behaviour as a result of experience, then the future of an advanced economic system can *never* exactly replicate the past, as it is frequently assumed in quantitative analysis to do. Of course, there are numerous other, non-human, disturbances which also tend to make the future different from the past.

Paradoxically, although the post-war development of quantitative methods has led to a much greater refinement of pure theory, it has led to a coarsening in the application of theory to the understanding of actual problems. On the application of economic theory to what he calls 'social questions', Johnson writes:

The central concepts of the relevant economic theory are, I believe, relatively simple and easy to grasp: the hard task, as every economist knows, is to recognise their relevance to particular problems, and apply them to finding solutions.[8]

There is no apparent reason why the precision of thinking introduced by quantitative methods should not have been applied to the 'art' of application as well as to the 'science' of theorizing in economics. That it has not done so is evident from a reading of journal articles in the past twenty years, where evidence of the crude and unthinking application of quantitative methods abounds, in defiance of the assumptions of statistics and economic theory alike. The most notable crudity is the treatment of *ex ante* theoretic relationships as if they could be captured by *ex post* observations.[9] The fact that the precision of thinking associated with quantitative methods can be used in the application of theory to policy problems is illustrated in some writings of contemporary economists. These are unfortunately rare exceptions to the rule. Contrary to what Johnson has written, it is evident from the pages of the scholarly journals that every economist does *not* know that it is a hard task to apply economic theory to finding solutions to particular problems in modern advanced economies.

The careless application of quantitative methods in economics can be attributed to the contemporary misunderstanding which associates the use of such methods with scientific procedure. As I shall show in greater detail in chapter 9, it is a misunderstanding to suppose that because quantitative methods constitute the greater part of scientific procedure in the natural sciences, they must do so in the social sciences too. I do not, however, share the view of Von Mises that quantitative analysis is appropriate only for the natural sciences, and *a priori* methods of reasoning are the only ones appropriate for the social sciences. I do believe that quantitative methods can usefully be applied in economics to the solution of a limited range of questions. However, the major questions of contemporary policy, such as those raised in this book, do not fall within this range. What I wish to emphasize is that, although a knowledge of magnitudes is important, the quantitative aspects of a phenomenon are neither its only nor necessarily its most important aspects. And, of course, recourse can be had to empirical evidence without the adoption of quantitative methods.

Narrowing effect of a limited choice of variables

One of the major consequences of the widespread adoption of quantitative methods in economics is that the range of variables and relationships admissible in theory and in application has been narrowed to those which are easily quantifiable and, within that range, to those which are thought to be purely 'economic'. In this connection, it is significant that in their criticism of the present state of economics, both Leontief and Phelps Brown are agreed that this narrowing process must be reversed, and that the scope of economic theory must be broadened to include social, political and psychological variables. Leontief suggests that analysis must 'reach unhesitatingly beyond the limits of the domain of economic phenomena as it has been stated up to now'. In similar vein, Phelps Brown writes: 'my argument implies a removal of the traditional boundary between the subject matter in economics and the other social sciences'.

As has only recently been recognized, one of the harmful consequences of the overemphasis on quantitative methods has been the misinterpretations placed upon Keynes's *General Theory*. In the course of its attempted quantification, a number of important elements have been effectively left out. One of these was expectations: there can be little doubt that this was because the famous Chapter Twelve on The State of Long Term Expectations did not lend itself easily to quantification.

Two other crude and unwarranted — yet widely accepted — interpretations of Keynes's *General Theory* have flowed from the predominance of quantitative methods. First, the preoccupation with quantifiable macro-aggregates has led post-war economists to overlook the fact that the behaviour of these variables are merely symptoms of the well-being or the ill-being of the economy: what a study of these variables cannot do is to identify the sources of that well-being or ill-being. Secondly, despite the fact that Keynes's theory was confined explicitly to a short-term situation in which even the capital stock of the society was assumed to be fixed, it led to the post-war growth 'theory', accepted by economists and civil servants alike, that demand expansion is the key to rapid economic growth. This belief has diverted attention from the possibility that such other policies as the set of relative prices, housing, the taxation of income, the composition of investment, policies concerning the labour-market, etc. might have an influence on the rate of growth.

This type of theorizing about economic growth, based upon an unwarranted and crudely quantified extension of Keynes's thinking, has led not only to the exclusion of the conventional micro-economic aspects of the process of economic growth, but much more importantly it has excluded the broad insights into the process of growth which the classical tradition of economic theorizing affords. In Johnson's words it:

> has . . . prevented [economists] from stretching their minds to comprehend the influence of social and cultural institutions on the efficiency and potential growth of the economy and the kinds of non-economic policies that might be useful in solving the country's problems

and

> it has occurred to very few economists indeed to examine whether cognate social scientists . . . and management and similar consultant experts have more to say than the economist about what kinds of changes in existing social and institutional arrangements are capable of increasing productivity.[10]

Thus, neglect of the classical tradition of thought on the subject of economic growth has been assisted by the Keynesian revolution.

Absence of a contemporary theory of economic growth

The shift in the *method* of inquiry of economics to a narrower, more quantitative basis has proceeded in parallel with a shift in the *subject-matter* of economics. The point of departure of this latter movement may be taken to be Ricardo's often-quoted letter to Malthus, in which he stated quite explicitly, and contrary to the classical tradition, that the principal purpose of economic inquiry should not be the study of economic growth but the study of distribution. Thus began a shift in mainstream economic thought in which less and less attention has been paid to the theory of value. Discussion of the theory of economic growth, at least in the context of the advanced economies, has languished for so long that it is safe to say that no proper theory of economic growth exists. It has been left to a handful of writers to contribute occasional essays which form largely isolated contributions. It is this situation which is lamented by Joan Robinson in the quotation on p. viii of this book.

In view of the proliferation of articles and books in the last thirty years which have included in their titles the words 'growth' and 'theory', it may seem at first quixotic or even reckless to claim that there does not exist a contemporary theory of economic growth. However, it was first pointed out many years ago that this literature (which we may identify as pertaining to the theory of steady-state growth) does not constitute a theory of economic growth in the proper sense. This is hardly surprising in view of its origins. On the neo-classical side, it is derived from a theory of value and, on the neo-Keynesian side, from a theory of employment.

'Steady-state' growth models do not constitute a theory of economic growth, because they offer no explanation or prediction of the way in which actual economies have developed or are likely to develop over time. For this reason, such models were quite rightly excluded by Abramowitz from his 1952 survey of the theory of economic growth for the American Economic Association.[11] When Hahn and Matthews came to the same task thirteen years later, they confined themselves *solely* to a survey of steady-state models. They recognized, in doing so, that the literature they were surveying was different from that 'which would be used if the *immediate* purpose was to provide the best available explanation of the variety of historical growth experience'.[12] They justified their choice of scope for their survey on the grounds of the increasing volume of this type of literature, and added rather lamely that 'the authors of these models have naturally had in mind as a rule that their work should contribute to an understanding of the way economies actually grow over time'. This enormously influential survey has appeared on countless undergraduate reading lists; yet none of these students would have been made aware by it of the contributions to the theory of economic growth which had been made by Sweezy or Schumpeter, to name but two.

In retrospect, few economists would doubt which writings made a greater contribution to 'an understanding of the way economies actually grow over time'. Not only has the 'arid formalism' of steady-state theory led nowhere, it can actually be seen to have made a negative contribution to the understanding of the growth process. It has led those economists whose concern is with actual advanced economies to regard growth as a smooth process, devoid of qualitative change. Although the flood of literature on steady-state growth theory has slowed to a trickle, no substantive contributions to the theory of economic growth have emerged for almost two decades. This is all the more remarkable when there have been perceptible changes in technology, institutions and attitudes in the advanced countries during this period, as well as changes in output, the price level and unemployment.

It is my contention that the essential feature of advanced economies is change, and that most of the major 'problems' which are perceived by economists and policy-makers in these countries represent adjustments to both exogenously and endogenously created changes. It is therefore difficult to arrive at a satisfactory understanding of these problems without a theory of economic growth.

There are therefore three distinct, but related, reasons for the failure of contemporary economic analysis to explain satisfactorily the problems of the advanced economies. The first is that its attention is largely confined to relationships which are easily quantifiable. The second is that contemporary economic analysis is confined to too narrow a set of variables; and thirdly, that it lacks a theory of economic growth.

Contemporary analysis is therefore misleading because it focuses on variables amenable to conventional economic reasoning rather than upon the determinants of social reality. Conventional reasoning has gone astray, because too many economists have inexplicably turned their backs on the foundations of their subject. Thus, not only are the most elementary propositions of neo-classical value theory disregarded, so that price is ignored as an explanatory factor in circumstances of excess supply in labour or foreign-exchange markets; much more seriously, the 'bedrock truths' about the human condition, first enunciated by classical political economy, have been forgotten.[13]

For present purposes, the latter is the more serious omission, since the problems of contemporary economics are problems of adjustment to change. Once we recognize this, we are dealing with the theme of economic progress in the long run which is the central question of classical political economy. 'No lesser intellectual framework will permit us usefully to serve our societies, and end the costly repetition of the inter-War irrelevance of mainstream economics', which has marked the post-war decades.[14]

4

The Classical Tradition in Growth Theory

In this chapter and in chapter 5, I shall set out the essential
elements of some classical theories of economic growth. In
doing so, my purpose is to establish similarities between the
contributions of different major writers, and thereby to
provide a perspective for the analysis of economic growth
which may be helpful in understanding contemporary problems. The present chapter concentrates on the general features
of selected writers and, in particular, on the role which they
assigned to institutions and attitudes as variables. Chapter 5
deals with the process of growth and, in particular, with the
extension of the division of labour.

Some justification is necessary for the assertion that the
economists I have selected can be said to belong to a single
tradition. I therefore begin by setting out six principles to
which all of them could subscribe, and which, despite their
own differences, clearly mark them off from the neo-classical
synthesis.[1]

For the classical economists, the central question of
economics was the growth of output, not the allocation of a
fixed quantity of resources.[2] The primacy of this question
for Smith is evident both from the title of his major work and
from the proportions of space within it allotted to what we
should nowadays call the theory of growth and the theory of
value. The classical tradition is, above all, concerned with the
evolution of economic systems, including endogenous changes
in institutions. Particular attention is paid to the historical,
cultural and political circumstances of the country concerned.

Secondly, all economists in the classical tradition recognize the importance of the human element in economic behaviour, in particular, the purposive nature of human action. This is in marked contrast to the neo-classical approach, of which it has been said that once the individual has left a picture of his tastes in the form of a set of indifference curves, he can disappear altogether. A definition of classical economics which succinctly incorporates these first two principles is provided by John Stuart Mill:

> Insofar as the economical condition of nations turns upon the state of physical knowledge, it is the subject of the physical sciences and the arts founded upon them. But insofar as the causes are moral or psychological, dependent upon institutions and social relations, or on the principles of human nature, their investigation belongs not to physical but moral and social science and is the object of what is called political economy.[3]

Third, in the classical view, the central feature of market economies is not that they exhibit tendencies towards equilibrium in various markets, but rather that they manifest continuous and endogenous change in all their principal variables. This is closely associated with the classical view of competition as a dynamic process involving qualitative technical change. Whereas the neo-classical analysis of the market mechanism leads to the conclusion that an increase in the demand for a commodity tends to result in an increase in its price, in Smith's view an increase in demand 'never fails' to lower the price of a good in the long run.[4]

Fourth, most writers in the classical tradition do not recognize disciplinary boundaries between economics and the other social sciences.

Fifth, most classical writers would agree that there is a qualitative difference between the satisfaction of human material needs, and the attempted satisfaction of human wants, which are in principle unlimited. This distinction between consumption behaviour which is close to the level of subsistence and that which is well above it has been swept away by neo-classical theory. The classical view would be that in the short run there is a rough proportionality between volume of consumption and satisfaction, but that in the long run there is what Galbraith has called 'a diminishing urgency of wants'. On the other hand, neo-classical analysis leads to the conclusion that there is a diminishing marginal utility from consumption in the short run, and that intertemporal comparisons of utility cannot be made.

Finally, classical economists tend to distinguish between categories of labour which are 'productive' and those which are 'unproductive'. This distinction, originated by the Physiocrats, emphasized by Smith, and preserved in the national accounts of the contemporary East European economies, has recently been revived by Bacon and Eltis. No such distinction is recognized in neo-classical analysis.

On questions of method, the classical tradition does not adopt a narrow view of what constitutes admissible criteria for reasoning or for empirical inquiry in economics. Although the classical economists shared the central objective of an increase in the annual material output of society, they did not always distinguish carefully between what we should nowadays call 'positive' and 'normative' analysis. On the other hand, although they dealt with such macro-variables as aggregate output, capital stock and the supply of labour, relations between them were soundly based on processes which operated at the level of the individual firm, that is, classical macro-economics had firm micro-foundations.

The principal figures who fall within the tradition and whose work is discussed in this chapter and the next include Adam Smith and some of his contemporaries, Marx, the Austrian school, Veblen and Schumpeter. Ricardo is left out, on account of his explicit denial of the primacy of the growth question,[5] although Malthus might have been included. The whole book II of Malthus's *Principles* is devoted to the problem of economic progress, but his only lasting contribution, the principle of population, is of little concern to the advanced countries of today.

Although few people would dispute the right of Marx to be included in the classical tradition, it may be asked what justification there is for admitting economists who wrote after 1871 to the classical tradition, as I have claimed to do. The answer must be that they should be admitted, if, by virtue of the scope and/or method of their work, they conform to the principles outlined at the beginning of this chapter. If Marx is admitted to the classical school, then so must the neo-Marxists. But how can Austrians and neo-Austrians be included in this tradition when Menger, the founder of the Austrian school, was himself an instigator of the 'marginal revolution'?

The fact is that acceptance of the marginal principle is almost the only thing which Austrians have in common with the contemporary neo-classical synthesis. In all other respects they adhere to the classical tradition. One of the strands in the Austrian tradition, descending from Menger to Von Mises, Hayek and Morgenstern, is the proclamation of the flimsiness of the foundations on which contemporary neo-classical macro-economic aggregates rest. A leading contemporary Austrian has gone so far as to write:

> Hardly an author can be found, not even Keynes himself, who is so much the exact antipode of Milton Friedman in every part of the economist's theoretical vision as Carl Menger.[6]

Despite the advance of neo-classical economics and the associated disappearance of the subject of economic growth from the mainstream of economic thought, a number of economists have continued to work in the spirit of the classical tradition. These include such neo-Marxists as Baran and Sweezy, neo-Austrians such as Lowe and Schumpeter, and other contemporaries such as Mishan, Hirsch and Heilbroner.

Classical theory of economic growth

It is helpful to begin with those colleagues and contemporaries of Adam Smith, members of the eighteenth-century enlighten-

ment, who first established theoretical links between economic and social organization. They are the forerunners of the
classical tradition in the theory of economic growth. These
writers[7] seem to have accepted Aristotle's dictum that:

> If you consider the state — or anything else for that matter
> — in relation to the origins from which it springs, you will
> arrive at the clearest understanding of its nature.[8]

Accordingly, they traced the development of human society
through stages, each of which was marked by distinctive institutional arrangements. The mechanism of progress was roughly
as follows: the driving forces for change were three basic
human attitudes: self-love, a desire for action and a desire to
improve the material conditions of life. Working out these
forces within a particular natural and institutional environment produces results beyond man's original intention[9] and
so produces a qualitatively changed environment within which
the same psychological propensities will continue to operate.
From this continuing process of economic development, these
writers concluded that there must be a constant process of
change in society itself.

They identified four stages of economic growth: the
primitive, the pastoral, the agricultural and the exchange
economy. In the first, there was no property, no need therefore for government, and inequality was based entirely on
non-economic factors. With the second stage, the pastoral,
comes the domestication of animals and hence the possibility
of the accumulation of capital, inequality in its distribution
and hence the need for government. In Smith's words, 'the
very end of government is to secure wealth and to defend the
rich from the poor'.[10]

The institution of property, in the view of the Scottish
historical school, is therefore both a divisive factor in society
and at the same time an essential instrument in the process of
economic growth.[11]

In the third and fourth stages of growth, property remains
but the nature of the relationship between economic and

social institutions changes. In the agrarian stage, the institution of property is consolidated: the principal asset, land, is less destructible and at the same time more unequally distributed than the principal asset, cattle, of the previous, pastoral stage. This means a lessening of freedom for the individual who does not possess property, dependent as he is for his subsistence upon the property owner. But the forces for change would eventually lead, through the creation of an agricultural surplus, to the development of commerce and manufactures; this development would ultimately undermine the agrarian economy, with its associated institutions, and lead to the final stage in the process of growth, the exchange economy. This last stage is characterized by a wider distribution of property, held increasingly in the form of industrial and commercial assets. Further, this stage will be marked by an increasing division of labour and therefore an increased inter-dependence. The creation of the market for labour services emancipates the non-property-owning individual from a feudal dependence on others and puts him in the position of a tradesman, who 'derives his subsistence from the employment not of one but of 100 or 1000 different customers. Though in some measure obliged to them all he is not absolutely dependent on any one of them.'[12]

Thus the historians of the Scottish enlightenment saw the exchange economy as the final stage of the process of economic growth, which first diminished individual liberty and then re-established it in a higher and qualitatively different form. Although these writers did entertain some doubts about what we might nowadays call the side-effects of the exchange economy, in particular, as Skinner says, that 'the division of labour might bring material benefits to the vast mass of mankind and simultaneously deprive them of the wit to enjoy these benefits',[13] they never doubted that the exchange economy was the only route to material improvement for the mass of the people. Not only did they not look to any alternative route, they did not look beyond the exchange-economy stage. This may have been because they were aware of the complexities of history and were disinclined to predict.

Adam Smith

Institutions were Adam Smith's prescription for successful economic development.[14] Smith shared the view that the exchange economy had evolved from a historical process; moreover, that it represented the highest form of institutional development, in the sense that it made possible the realization of adequate material living standards for the entirety of the large and indeed expanding population, while at the same time permitting a greater degree of political freedom than had hitherto been known.[15] Whether this potential for economic growth could be realized effectively would depend upon the 'correct' choice of the institutional framework by the political sovereign. The central purpose of the *Wealth of Nations* is to prescribe the framework most suitable for a country such as Great Britain, embarking upon the exchange economy as a stage of its development. The unchanging propensities of human nature, operating within that framework consciously designed by political choice, would produce a process of continuing economic growth. The details of this process of growth within the stage of the exchange economy are discussed in the following chapter. For the moment it is sufficient to note that Smith's analysis was heavily influenced by Newtonian mechanics, though it has nothing of the rigidities of modern steady-state 'growth' theories.[16]

What is important for the present purpose is that neither Smith nor his contemporaries looked beyond the stage of the exchange economy, which represented for them the ultimate form of institutional development. Within that stage, they sought to identify laws of human behaviour corresponding to the laws of the behaviour of the heavenly bodies which Newton had apparently identified with success. Thus, in his analysis of the process of growth within the exchange-economy stage, Smith was able to treat institutional, psychological and natural-resource parameters as given: 'being neither influenced by the ongoing core process nor subject to further historical development, these factors can be treated as genuine constants of the analysis'.[17]

Smith's institutional recipe for economic growth consisted of a system of competitive markets under the protection of a constitutional government whose principal duties consisted in the maintenance of law and order. So far as economic activity was concerned, the most important laws were those guaranteeing individual freedom, freedom of contract and the protection of private property. The system then operates according to the twin principles of free exchange and the division of labour. It is worth repeating that it is growth of output, not the efficient allocation of a given stock of resources, which is Smith's principal justification for these institutional arrangements.

Smith believed that there were certain 'unchanging and universal principles of human nature', that is, that there were certain fundamental motives which were constant in time and place. The first of these was material self-interest or the desire to better one's own condition (which obviously combines the first and the third motives of the Scottish historical school). This is by far the most important motive in Smith's theory of economic development, leading Lowe to give it the title of 'The Universal Pecuniary Motive'. It is certainly the driving force of the exchange-economy stage. The ambition to acquire wealth, prestige and power drives many individuals to make extraordinary efforts. So far as the individual is concerned, the objectives remain illusory and their attainment results only in 'more fatigue of body and more uneasiness of mind'. But from the point of view of society as a whole, the delusions induced by ambition are highly beneficial:

it is this deception which rouses and keeps in continual motion the industry of mankind. It is this which first prompted them to cultivate the ground, to build houses, to found cities and commonwealths, and to invent and improve all the sciences and arts which ennoble and embellish human life; which have entirely changed the whole face of the globe, have turned the nude forests of nature into agreeable and fertile plains, and made the trackless and barren ocean a new fund of subsistence, and the great high road of communications to the different nations of the earth.[18]

On the other hand, in his other main work, *The Theory of Moral Sentiments*, Smith put forward a quite different motive as being the principal guiding force in human society. This was that men's behaviour was governed by a desire to enlist the sympathy of the impartial spectator. Thirdly, Smith recognized in the *Wealth of Nations* the existence of a universal human propensity to 'truck and barter'.

In addition to these three fundamental motives of human behaviour, Smith recognized a number of ways in which attitudes entered into the process of economic development, influencing other variables and, in turn, being influenced by them. There were the tendencies towards rationalization, which Smith recognized as being introduced by an exchange economy: 'whenever commerce is introduced into any country, probity and punctuality always accompany it'. In this may be seen an early recognition of the process of standardization, which is perhaps one of the central characteristics of economic growth in the advanced countries. Fifth, Smith regarded parsimony as being of critical importance in the process of the accumulation of capital (he made no distinction between saving and investment).[19] A sixth factor which Smith identified was the urge to procreate.

Next, Smith shared with his compatriots of the Scottish historical school the perception that the specialization of function, which was at the heart of the process of development in an exchange economy, would be accompanied by increasing alienation as well as by inequality. It was for the former reason that Smith advocated a system of public education, in the hope of offsetting the narrowing effects of the division of labour. As to inequality, he was well aware not only that government was necessary for the protection of property but that property is necessarily accompanied by inequality: 'wherever there is a great property there is great inequality'.[20]

So far as the utility of consumption is concerned, it is clear from the *Theory of Moral Sentiments* that Smith did not believe that beyond a certain point personal material improvement would lead to a commensurate increase in satisfaction. In general terms, he disapproved of excessively high consumption on both moral and social grounds.[21]

Later writers attached great importance to the entrepreneur as a special type; Smith did not do this, presumably believing that much the same characteristics were present in all human beings. Smith favoured partnerships, and was suspicious of the joint-stock company, though he recognized its necessity for large-scale capital enterprises.

Karl Marx

Marx inherited from Smith and the Scottish historical school an evolutionary view of human institutions, in which property played a decisive role. His distinctive contribution to the theory of economic growth was to look beyond the supposedly final stage of the exchange economy and to see in what way the historical process would evolve further in terms of economic and political institutions. Writing some seventy-five years later than Smith, Marx saw the exchange economy – or capitalism, as he called it – as being not the ultimate, but the penultimate, stage of institutional development. He predicted that it would eventually give way to a new stage, socialism, in which property would be owned by the community in the form of the state and in which stage, therefore, there would be the need for neither government nor inequality. Unlike Smith, Marx devoted very little time to an analysis of the institutional arrangements and the behavioural characteristics of his ultimate stage.[22] As the title of his major work suggests, by far the greater part of his effort was devoted to analysing the exchange economy, and the way in which it would be transformed into socialism. The essential ideas are by now familiar. During the period of capitalism, the process of competition between owners of capital will lead to the concentration of ownership in fewer and fewer hands. At a certain point, when the discrepancy in wealth and income between the property-owning few and the property-less many becomes politically intolerable, there is a violent upheaval and ownership of the entire stock of capital passes into the hands of the state, which, having previously been the instrument of the few, now becomes the instrument of the many. In neither stage, however, are the political institutions representative or democratic. In the exchange-economy stage, the stage is merely 'the executive committee of the bourgeoisie', whereas, in the socialist stage, it becomes 'the dictatorship of the proleteriat'. The point at which the transition from exchange economy to socialism takes place is the one at which a sufficiently large capital stock has been accumulated, so that most (if not all) commodities can be produced at zero cost. The system of markets as an institution for allocating resources is therefore replaced by a planning system, but its mode of operation, like so much else in the socialist stage, is left unspecified.

All of Marx's essential ideas on the subject of growth are contained in the *Communist Manifesto*, published in 1849. His subsequent work, in particular the three volumes of *Capital*, were simply devoted to fleshing these ideas out. It is unfortunate, however, that Marx did not attempt an analysis of the socialist stage, and this subject, apparently ripe for analysis or speculation by scholars, has been strangely neglected. Supposing this stage to be realized, what institutional arrangements, attitudes and economic processes will or should prevail within it? Again, supposing it to have been reached, what are some of the tendencies present in the economic and social forces at work within it which will cause it to give way to a further stage of institutional development? And what might the characteristics of this further stage be? Scholars may plausibly claim that it is too early to undertake such studies, but it is surely quite unscientific to suppose that history will come to a stop at one stage. Changes in technology are but one of the many potential sources of continuous change which may have implications for institutions and for human behaviour generally.

Although the members of the Scottish historical school were well aware of the complexities of history, and would regard their account of institutional development as having all the simplicities of a model, with all the qualifications which that implies in terms of its applicability to the real world, Marx had no such scruples or sense of subtlety. His crude historical determinism, his equally crude materialism, the assertion that ownership of property is the sole criterion of the transitions through historical stages, the assertion that property is the only source of inequality, and so on, represent a dogmatization of earlier theories. Whatever this gains in ideological appeal, it is diminished in scholarly respectability and no doubt accounts for the fact that for so long Marx's contribution has not been taken seriously by economists, despite his impeccable classical credentials. Despite all these defects, and despite the fact that Marx, with the virtue of hindsight, may be seen to have been wrong in almost every detail, there can be little doubt that Schumpeter is right when he says that Marx's 'vision' is correct: namely, that there are tendencies clearly discernible in advanced economies which have been moving them away from a set of institutions which we can call the exchange economy or the market economy or capitalism, and in the direction of another set of institutions which broadly fit the label of socialism. This is not to say that these tendencies may not be arrested, diverted or even reversed, but it would be idle to pretend that they did not exist and indeed that they do not play a major part in the working of contemporary advanced economies.

As we have seen, Marx adopted and amended in his own way the earlier 'stage' theories of economic development and focused his particular attention upon the same stage as did Adam Smith, that is, the exchange-economy stage or, in Marx's words, the stage of 'capitalism'. In this stage there were two principal groups of agents, the bourgeoisie and the workers. The working class in this stage are depicted in Gray's words as 'a race of economic men' devoid of any passions or of any human characteristics other than an instinct for class 'solidarity'.[23] Although Marx shared with the other members of

the classical tradition the belief that human beings act purposefully, there is an important difference of emphasis between
him and the later Austrian school. Marx believed that only
collective consciously planned behaviour matters, whereas the
Austrians believed that it is the unintended consequences of
individual action which are frequently decisive. The Austrians
were also subjectivists, whereas Marx was a materialist.

The other contenders in Marx's vision of the capitalist
stage were the bourgeoisie, that is, the owners of capital.
They, too, were one-dimensional men; they were moved solely
by a passion for accumulation or a 'werewolf thirst for profits'.
Despite his colourful language, Marx may have been closer to
the truth than later economists in attributing to capitalists in
nineteenth-century England the motivation of accumulation
for its own sake, or out of 'animal spirits'. The foundations
of a family dynasty may have seemed a greater ambition than
the enlightened pursuit of rational material gain (that is,
profit maximization), which can be perhaps more appropriately attributed to the salaries of managers of joint-stock
companies rather than to the self-employed partners in a
family firm.

Marx followed Smith in recognizing that the dynamic
process of capitalism is a cosmopolitanizing force. 'To the
despair of reactionaries', writes Marx, 'it has cut from under
the feet of industry its national basis, so that national narrow-
ness and exclusiveness have become daily more and more
impossible'. It has also rescued a great part of the population
from what Marx described as 'the idiocy of country life'.

However, unlike Smith, Marx seems to have been an out-
and-out materialist. There is no indication of any awareness
or acceptance of a diminishing utility of consumption, or
even a diminishing urgency of wants. It may be significant
that the final stage of communism is characterized by an
abundance of material goods.

The Austrian school

Menger, the founder of the Austrian school, pointed out that major institutions of human societies, such as markets and money, religion, law, language and even the state itself, came into existence through human action, but not through human design. He claims that this is so because such institutions are first encountered in periods of history 'where we cannot properly speak of a purposeful activity of the community'.[24]

Menger uses the word 'organic' to refer to institutions generated by such processes, as opposed to 'pragmatic' phenomena which are the results of legislation or conscious collective agreement. He felt that the earlier classical economists had missed this important distinction: 'what Adam Smith and his followers can actually be charged with is . . . their defective understanding of the unintentionally created social institutions and their significance for the economy'.[25] Elsewhere, Menger is quoted as having observed: 'How is it possible that institutions which serve the common welfare and are the most important for its advancement can arise without a common will aiming at their creation?' To a modern Austrian, this is still 'the significant, perhaps the most significant problem, of the social sciences'.[26] In a similar vein, Popper writes that only a minority of social institutions are consciously designed whereas the vast majority have just 'grown' as the undesigned results of human action' and, he continues, 'social institutions may emerge as unintended consequences of rational actions'.[27] Hayek writes that the outstanding problem of the social sciences is to create a 'composite theory of social phenomena' in order to 'grasp how the independent actions of many men can produce coherent wholes, persistent structures or relationships *which serve important human purposes* without having been designed for that end' (my italics).[28]

This, then, is the Austrian view of the nature of institutions. As explanations of the origin of institutions they reject unequivocally, and in my view rightly, the doctrines of pragmatism, historical determinism and behaviourism. Most Austrians, notably Hayek and Von Mises (but not Schumpeter and Lowe), seem to share Adam Smith's view that the exchange economy is the highest form of institutional development which is available to advanced societies. It is not that they deny that such an economy might one day be replaced by socialism: it is simply that they feel that such a step would be accompanied not only by a significant loss of material output (through allocative inefficiency) but, more importantly, it would be inevitably accompanied by a significant loss of political freedom.[29] Being subjectivists and individualists, the Austrian school attach great importance to the role of attitudes in economic activity. In a world of uncertainty, that is, a world in which knowledge is dispersed or inadequate, Austrians believe that it is necessary to take account of the way in which people differ according to their (a) expectations about future events and behaviour, (b) knowledge of their own tastes as well as of the opportunities available to them, (c) interpretation of current events and the actions of others, and (d) alertness to new opportunities previously unperceived. Above all, Austrians believe that individuals act purposefully and agree with Adam Smith that there are indeed universal characteristics of human nature (such as a propensity for self-betterment), but differ sharply with him and with Marx over the possibility of collective choice. However, they also believe that there is an indeterminacy and unpredictability inherent in human preferences, human expectations and human knowledge, and that the act of choice is frequently spontaneous and creative.

It may be noteworthy that, although the Austrians appear to have dissected elegantly the motives of agents and the processes of the exchange economy, they do not seem to have paid as much attention to the internal modes of operation of large private corporations as well as public-sector bureaucracies.[30] Together these organizations are responsible for allocating a large proportion of total national output in the advanced countries.

The American institutionalists

The leading figures of the American institutionalist school (Veblen, Mitchell, Commons, Ayres) are located in time between the 'early' Austrians, such as Menger, and the 'later' Austrians, such as Hayek. Whereas the Austrian school of thought survives, indeed flourishes, the American institutional school has sunk without trace, unless Galbraith can be counted as a late member. Although it may seem as if the two schools have little in common, and indeed Veblen's first published articles could be interpreted as an attack on the method of Menger and of the classical school, in fact both schools have a similar view of the evolution of institutions and of economic activity, which is wholly in line with the classical tradition.

Like Smith and his Scottish contemporaries and Marx, Veblen thought in terms of the development of society through stages. He distinguishes four: savagery, barbarism, the era of handicrafts and the age of machine technology. As Seckler says, 'Veblen at times felt that contemporary technology may occasion a drift to socialism', but he refused to take a deterministic view. Veblen's view of the way in which institutions evolve was summarized by Wesley Mitchell in the following terms: 'as ways of working shift, they will engender new habits of thinking which will crystallise into new institutions, which will form the cultural setting for further accumulative changes in ways of working . . .'[31]

Veblen's idea of capitalism, being associated with the handicraft era (that is, with small units of production and with malleable and mobile capital) accords with the circumstances of the time in which Adam Smith wrote and, it must be said, with the assumptions of factor mobility which underlie neo-classical value theory. In an era in which production is organized significantly in large-scale units and in which capital is formed into large and specific lumps, it may be argued that machine technology can be associated with the stage of socialism. If indeed the present-day economies of the advanced countries can be characterized in this way, then this may, in part, explain the failure of government to allow Rolls Royce, British Leyland, Lockheed or Chrysler to collapse, and the British government compelling its electricity generating boards to buy power stations they do not need and do not want in order to provide continuity of employment. In the same way, the pressures for high US defence and space spending may not be so much military as political and economic in origin. The famous US military and industrial complex may not be fuelled so much by the profit motives of arms dealers and manufacturers as by the trade unions' desire for continuity of employment. The same reasons may explain the otherwise strange anxiety of leftist governments in advanced countries to attract inward investment by multinational companies.

Joseph Schumpeter

Following Veblen, Schumpeter was the next major figure in the classical tradition to analyse the phenomenon of growth in an advanced economy. He did this first in his *Theory of Economic Development*, published in the year 1912. Schumpeter saw growth in the capitalist stage as being inseparably linked to fluctuations and as being sectorally unbalanced. Fluctuations arise because of qualitative changes which come in clusters and disturb the cyclical flow of activity. These changes are innovations, the introduction of new products and of new techniques which will cluster together and cause an upward surge of investment and thus enforced saving. The capitalist plays a heroic role in the growth of the market economy. This entrepreneur innovator is to be distinguished carefully from the routine manager co-ordinating the factors of production, as in the neo-classical analysis. When the investment boom is over, there follows a recession of output and prices which wipes out the non-viable innovations and the inferior imitations. Thus Schumpeter's theory of growth is a dynamic one, a series of disturbances to the otherwise smooth flow of economic activity.

It is not difficult to find in Schumpeter the influence of Marxist thinking: indeed in his later work, *Capitalism, Socialism and Democracy* (first published in 1942), he expressly approved the correctness of the Marxist vision that capitalism would be replaced eventually by socialism. He also followed

Marx in believing that this change would be brought about by factors endogenous to the capitalist system itself, although he advanced very different reasons from Marx for the disappearance of capitalism. Schumpeter summarily rejects Marx's criterion of ownership; nor does he show any interest in the criterion of income distribution. For him, the key indicator in the transition from capitalism to socialism is *state control* of the forms of economic organization, whether carried out by legislation, taxation or by public ownership. The critical watershed in this transition is 'the socialisation of the labour market'. Schumpeter defined capitalism as 'a scheme of values, an attitude towards life, a civilisation – the civilisation of inequality and the family fortune'. He posed three types of questions concerning growth in the advanced countries: first, what is the nature of growth under the capitalist system? Second, can capitalism survive? Third, if not, what kind of socialism would follow it? Will it be workable and will it be compatible with democracy?

The steady and gradual decomposition of capitalism is, in Schumpeter's view, due to a 'quenching of capitalist attitudes and institutions'. The interaction of the different influences is subtle, but they arise from within the system itself. This idea has echoes of Marx's idea that capitalism carries within itself the seeds of its own destruction, but whereas in Marx's case destruction comes about in an abrupt and violent collision between material and political forces, in Schumpeter's view destruction is slow and moves through intangibles: the transition is painless, and indeed the date of transition may not be clearly marked. In both cases, however, capitalism is destroyed by its own success.

The biggest single factor in the decline of capitalism is the decline in the motivation of the entrepreneur. The modern corporation, though a product of the capitalist process, socializes the bourgeois mind. It relentlessly narrows the scope of capitalist motivation; not only that, it will eventually kill its roots. The modern corporation businessman is of the executive type; he acquires something of the psychology of the salaried employee working in a bureaucratic organization.

The increasing concentration of the size of the firm means that the political structure of society is profoundly changed (as Marx had predicted) by the elimination of a host of small and medium-sized firms. Size also knocks out the notion of property or of freedom of contract; the figure of the proprietor, and with it the specifically proprietary interest, vanishes from the picture. The labour contract is impersonal, stereotyped and bureaucratic. 'The capitalist process takes the life out of the idea of property'.[32]

In his last paper, which was left uncompleted at his death, Schumpeter listed four major psychological characteristics of the transition of capitalism to socialism, as follows:

1   The standard of living created by the business class undermines the social and political position of that class: their task becomes ripe for bureaucratization.
2   In the capitalist firm it was loyalty which assured obedience to command. An employment arrangement which is based on contract only cannot work.
3   A bureaucratic class has been created which, together with the workers, 'raids' the business class.
4   Capitalist values lose their hold on public attitudes and even on the capitalist himself.

According to Schumpeter, the principal factor destroying capitalism was its 'underlying cast of mind', namely rational, sceptical and calculating. As Heilbroner writes: 'such a mind served capitalism well when its rise was opposed by the "irrational" privileges of an aristocratic order, but, once in the saddle, the critical intellectuality would be turned against the pretentions of property and would reveal them to be as empty as those of nobility'. Rationalism means the tendency to eliminate all non-rational influences in economic life — those based on custom, belief and loyalty. All the major writers in the classical tradition have noted the association between the growth of rationalism and economic progress. In Schumpeter's view, rationalism provides a continuum, according to which the transition from capitalism to socialism is unmarked by any discontinuity. Although the intangible and non-rational factors are the important ones in life, rationalism has spread outside the economic sphere and may account for the decline of conventional religious belief.[33]

Schumpeter believes that a transition from capitalism to socialism is probable. In a mature economy, according to Schumpeter, this transition presents no problem: the end of capitalism is heralded by the gradual transformation of attitudes and institutions favourable to socialism; there is usually an efficient bureaucracy already in place. However, when the essence of capitalist civilization – inequality and the family firm – has passed away, we still expect the golden eggs to be laid. When we are disappointed, says Schumpeter, we may find that centralist command socialism is a preferable alternative to the burdens of castrated capitalism. Schumpeter's prediction may be taken all the more seriously since he makes no secret of the fact that such a transition would be distasteful to him personally. He writes, 'personally, I prefer other cultural patterns'.[34]

5

Division of Labour and the Process of Change

This chapter discusses the essential features of the process of economic growth in a market economy as perceived by those writers whom we have designated as being in the classical tradition. These features include the continuous and qualitative nature of change, the significance of the division of labour and the nature of competition.

There can be little doubt that, in the classical view, the primary characteristic of the market economy is change. Not just quantitative change in a fixed range of goods produced by a fixed technology to satisfy fixed tastes, but continuous qualitative as well as quantitative change in all the variables. Marx observed that 'Constant revolutionising of production, the uninterrupted disturbance of social conditions, everlasting uncertainty and agitation distinguish the capitalist epoch from all earlier ones.'[1] More simply, Shackle notes that the market economy 'dissolves the settled conditions of life for ordinary people'.[2] Although change is a necessary condition of economic progress, it may be that it is precisely its disturbing nature which is at the heart of political opposition to the market economy.

In attempting to explain the process of change, members of the Scottish historical school started from the position that the constant principles of human nature operated within a constantly changing environment. In the words of Hume, 'It is universally acknowledged there is a great uniformity among the actions of men, in all nations and ages, and that human nature remains still the same in its principles and operations.' As Skinner writes, 'they argued that man, in following his natural propensities, inevitably produces results well beyond his original intention; that man, in reacting to a particular situation, must ultimately produce a qualitative change, thus creating a new situation within which the same forces must operate'. As we have seen, the Scottish historical school went on to establish connections between types of economic organization and types of social and political structure. From this they concluded that, given the constant process of economic development, there must be a constant process of change in society itself.

As we have seen earlier, all members of the classical tradition except one have been careful to avoid the suggestion that these changes in society brought about by the growth of the market economy are predictable. Only Marx adopted historical determinism in its pure form. The others would be likely to agree with T. S. Ashton who wrote: 'I do not want to see history written as though its function was simply to exhibit the gradualness of inevitability', and 'it is not true that everything rolls on to a predetermined end under the dynamics (whatever that means) of an impersonal force known as capitalism'.

The importance of the qualitative factor in economic growth was emphasized by Adam Smith when he stated that the two principal determinants of the annual output of a country were its supply of labour and the productivity of that labour. Whereas the neo-classical treatment of the concept of productivity empties it of all qualitative significance, and thus reduces the statement that gross output = quantity of labour x productivity of labour to an accounting identity, Smith had something more substantial in mind. By productivity, he meant 'the skill, dexterity, and judgement with which . . . labour is generally applied'.[3]

Corresponding to these two determinants of annual output, there were two complementary routes by which annual output might be increased. First, by a widening of the market, thus permitting an enhanced productivity of labour through the extension of the division of labour. Secondly, by expanding the supply of labour through an increase in the accumulation of capital.

Although scholars have differed as to which route constituted, in Smith's opinion, the more important mainspring of growth, this difference is of little significance, since the two mechanisms complement each other. Expanding the division of labour would normally be associated with the accumulation of capital through the introduction of new machinery, whereas the efficacy of a greater supply of labour in increasing productivity depends upon the extension of the division of labour.

Division of labour

It is, however, the emphasis which Smith placed upon the extension of the division of labour which is perhaps his principal contribution to the theory of economic growth. According to Allyn Young, Smith's theory of the division of labour is the 'most illuminating and fruitful generalisation found anywhere in the whole literature of economics'.[4] Von Mises is equally admiring: 'the fundamental fact that enabled man to elevate his species above the levels of the beasts and the horrors of biological competition was the discovery of the principle of the higher productivity of co-operation under a system of the division of labour, that great cosmic principle'.[5]

The key element in the increasing productivity realized by the extension of the division of labour is increasing organizational specialization, that is, an increase in the degree of roundaboutness. For example, the farmer has ceased to be his own butcher and baker, and a whole complex of 'agribusiness' industries has grown, supplying the inputs to and increasing the outputs of agriculture. Thus an extension of the division of labour is masked by the creation of new functions, which often, but not always, are associated with the establishment of new firms to carry them out. Many scholars have wondered why Smith chose the pre-industrial process of pin-making as the example with which to illustrate his division of labour principle, when the new Carron Iron Works were not far away. It has been suggested by Hollander, and appears most plausible, that by so doing he was able to exclude the influence of capital accumulation and techno-logical progress on rising productivity, and thus emphasize the importance of functional specialization.

The second most important thing about the division of labour is that it is limited by the extent of the market. So far as the internal market is concerned, rising income is a balancing force which reinforces itself through a spiral process. As with the supply of the factors, so with the supply of 'productivity': a rising aggregate output is both the consequence and the cause of its own increase. As for the external market, this accounts for the 'search for markets' which, in Young's view, unifies economic theory and economic history: 'no other single factor has a better claim to a leading role as the single explanatory factor of the industrial revolution'.[6]

Nowadays, we should be inclined to think that the rate of capital accumulation and the rate of progress of technology were more important determinants of the rate of growth of output than either the expansion of external markets or the extension of the division of labour. But this may be because the nature of economic growth in the advanced countries in the last quarter of the twentieth century is different from what it was in the same countries in the second half of the nineteenth century.

It is clear that Smith himself did not attach great import-ance to the rate of progress of technology. In his view, access to a passive flow of technical inventions was governed by the rate of accumulation, and the degree of the division of labour would adjust itself to this. Smith did not suspect that the rate of progress of technology could be accelerated by government intervention. Nor did it occur to him that the progress of technology would be sufficient to postpone indefinitely the arrival of the stationary state.

Smith seemed unaware that exchange in a non-barter economy involved an important element of uncertainty. On a self-sufficient farm expectations are limited to the weather and do not affect decision-making, because all other actions depend on one's own family's behaviour. However, the greater the extent to which the division of labour is carried, the more one is dependent on other people's decisions. Thus, as the market economy expands, the element of uncertainty must be increased, as an agent is drawn into a degree of dependence on others increasingly remote from his knowledge, let alone control, over a wider and wider range of transactions. Thus one is forced to form expectations about the behaviour of others before making one's own decisions. Here is where the social core to the economic process becomes vital. It is also perhaps a partial explanation as to why the advanced market economy may not be functioning properly.

Alienation is created by the division of labour, as Smith himself recognized. The narrowing effect was to be countered by state education. There seems to be no connection at all between the form of ownership and alienation. Indeed, Weil asserts that workers who work for a long time in one setting come to feel a need for ownership of the property concerned. Although it may be true that nowadays the brutalization induced by repetitive functions can be relieved by automation, there is no doubt surely that growth by specialization has smashed emotional bonds and has reduced links between people in production to cash ones. This, again, is not connected with the question of ownership.

The institutional framework prescribed by Smith has allowed free play to market forces which have driven millions of unskilled peoples from the countryside into the industrial towns of the advanced countries, from one town to another and even from one country to another. In this process, people were abruptly cut off from their religious, cultural and social roots. Perhaps the subsequent discontents and myths of exploitation can be explained more easily by the loss of such intangibles, including status, than by material losses. In this connection, Weil's metaphor of the stomach wound may be appropriate.

Inequality, in Smith's view, really arises from the distribution of property and not directly from specialization or division of labour. Nevertheless, the distribution of property itself is influenced by the progress of the division of labour. Inequality, in turn, causes pride and envy, the principal driving forces behind the great political movements of right and left, respectively, in the advanced countries.

As we have seen, in direct contrast to the neo-classical analysis, Smith believes that an increase in demand 'never fails' to lower the price of a good in the long run.[7] One thinks nowadays of cars and consumer electronic goods, to say nothing of computers. It does so because competition between producers is the force that drives manufacturers and merchants to seek out, develop and exploit the inexhaustible opportunities provided by the economies of scale and specialization. In other words, producers compete with each other through cost-cutting innovations of organization as well as of machinery and technology. In the neo-classical literature, on the other hand, such changes are treated as external economies of scale.

Nature of competition

Adam Smith's analysis of the effect of the division of labour on price, with its emphasis on competition driving down costs in the long run, as a result of increasing specialization within the industry, for the production of a commodity whose demand is increasing, clearly foreshadows a Marxist analysis of the process of competition between capitalists. In the Marxist analysis, emphasis is placed upon technological progress making possible successive cost-cutting innovations on the part of individual capitalists.[8] As a consequence, ownership of capital is concentrated in fewer and fewer hands. Leaving aside the question of the increasing concentration of ownership of capital, it does seem that the basic idea of competition through cost-cutting innovations of technology and of reorganization described by Smith and

Marx still provides a more satisfactory account of the essential nature of the market economy than do any of its neo-classical counterparts.

This classical vision of the nature of competition is shared by the Austrian school. It would not be unreasonable to suggest that all Austrian economics is the economics of growth. For them the passage of time is of central importance. Such concepts as uncertainty, imperfect knowledge, expectations and learning, which are an integral part of their economic analysis, are all related to the passage of time. In the neo-classical analysis of the market mechanism, a determinate solution can be obtained at a point of time when consumers' preferences and incomes are supposed to be known, as are the quality and the number of the goods. Buyers' and sellers' plans coincide.

The Austrians see the market as a process which takes place over time, characterized by an initial lack of knowledge, and therefore lack of co-ordination, and by learning leading to increasing co-ordination. A key Austrian view is that different people know different things: the market process gathers and transmits these discrete and often contradictory pieces of information. By drawing attention to, and remedying, the initial lack of co-ordination, competition acts as an equilibrating force.[9]

Since all action in the real world takes place in the face of more or less uncertainty, all action contains an element of entrepreneurship. This term refers to the alertness to profit opportunities not so far grasped by other market participants.[10] Accordingly, Austrians view a monopoly position as being only temporary, and describe monopoly profit as entrepreneurial profits, since it arises from successful exploitation of an opportunity which others have not yet seen. Like other Austrians, Schumpeter emphasized that the real source of competition to all firms, whether 'competitive' or 'monopolistic', arises not from other producers of the same product using the same technique, but from the producers of new and better products and/or techniques. Hence the market is characterized by a 'perennial gale of creative destruction'.

The parallel here with the Marxist and Smithian view of the market process is very clear.

Although the refinement of the neo-classical theory of value has been one of the central preoccupations of economists throughout the twentieth century, quite inhibiting the development of a theory of growth, J. M. Clark has pointed out that the analysis of static equilibrium should properly not be an end in itself, but should only be an introduction to the study of dynamics.[11] He advocates that the time sequences involved in the initiation of changes and adjustments to them, including expectations and uncertainties, should be introduced into demand and cost relationships. Clark recognizes that the transition to a dynamic theory of the market process can only be made at the price of sacrificing a determinate equilibrium, but this is a price worth paying, if it leads to the recognition that departures from the normative ideal of 'perfect' competition may be inseparable from progress. In Clark's view, the essence of competition is that competitive pressures make not only for the diffusion of gains from increased productivity, but also for the innovation and diffusion of new products.

6

What has happened in the Advanced Economies

Introduction

Although it is fashionable for some economic historians to deny that any formula for economic development exists, the fact is that those societies which have adopted the classical prescription for economic development set out by Smith and Marx have achieved spectacular progress in their material living standards. Yet this very success has undermined the institutions and attitudes which are necessary for the system to work satisfactorily. In Schumpeter's words:

> Capitalism, whilst economically stable, and even gaining in stability, creates, by rationalising the human mind, a mentality and style of life incompatible with its own fundamental conditions, motives, and social institutions, and will be changed, although not by economic necessity and probably even at some sacrifice of economic welfare, into an order of things which it will be merely a matter of taste and terminology to call Socialism or not.[1]

Our contemporary taste is to use the term 'the mixed economy'; the prospects for its survival are discussed in the next chapter. In this chapter, we examine some of the ways in which 'the order of things' has changed from the untrammelled market economy of the late nineteenth century. We begin with an account of the salient features of the market economy in its purest form, with private ownership of productive capital.

It is reasonable to suppose that in most, if not all, of the advanced countries there existed a period in their history in which the prevailing institutions and attitudes were sufficiently similar to those presumed to exist by Smith and by Marx that much of the theorizing in the classical and neo-classical traditions had a certain validity, especially concerning the theory of value. Thus, in the United Kingdom, from the early eighteenth to the late nineteenth century the economy did possess many of the characteristics which Adam Smith postulated, in terms of institutions, attitudes and behaviour. Accordingly, for some time the UK economy followed the type of growth pattern analysed by Smith, through the mechanism of the division of labour, and resources were allocated according to a roughly competitive market mechanism. In this 'classical' period, ownership of productive capital was in private hands and the predominant form of organization was the small family firm. Intervention in the economy, let alone control by government, was minimal, whether that intervention was in the form of regulation or of taxation. Government ownership of the means of production, too, was virtually non-existent. The role of government was confined to defence, the provision of a certain minimum infrastructure and, much later, education. The economy was made up of artisans, merchants and farmers, each possessing small units of labour-augmented capital. Technical and occupational substitution and the mobility of both labour and capital was thereby ensured. Only in the later stages of the Industrial Revolution did large lumps of highly product-specific capital become accumulated. Until then, investments did not involve large sums of capital nor long payback periods. In this pre-industrial period, investment and savings were identical. The general climate of confidence in progress helped to shape expectations favourably, although it should be noted that Smith quite failed to anticipate the cyclical fluctuations which were later analysed by Marx. Law and order, personal liberty, freedom of contract and the protection of private property were all upheld by the state. For the reasons explained by Smith, theft was considered a greater crime than violence, so that people were hanged for sheep-stealing. For those endowed with income-earning abilities, the prevailing ethos was that of self-help and personal material advancement. For those who were not, the need for survival in the face of market forces drove them to particular locations and to particular occupations. An urban proletariat was created, partly by the displacement of part of the rural-artisan population, but more importantly by an increase in the size of the population, which resulted, in turn, from the prior growth of output. The prevailing spirit of the age has been described as 'heroic materialism'.

Until the later nineteenth century, rising living standards were accompanied by rising birth-rates and falling death-rates, as proposed by the classical economists. Except for the very few, levels of consumption were not far above subsistence, and discussions about the problems of plenty did not arise. Initially, natural resources proved to be a constraint on growth: but with the reduction of transatlantic freight rates, the margin of agricultural production moved to Canada. A sufficient supply of capital was forthcoming to be exported, opening up additional supplies of raw materials and markets for British goods as well as direct investment overseas, which was only remotely related to the domestic economy, for example, British investment in railways and tramways in South America and Portugal. There is not much doubt that output, population, capital stock and output per head rose throughout the nineteenth century in the UK, if somewhat unsteadily. It rose later but faster in other countries, so that by 1914 both Germany and the United States had already overtaken the UK in output per head. There was, again, an unsteady stream of inventions, discoveries and innovations; colonial territories were 'opened up' by European powers. At the same time, there remained a significant rural population, marked fluctuations of economic activity, relative prices being flexible downwards with a steady general price level. Until the end of the nineteenth century, collective purposive action in the sphere of economic activity was slight.

Since the end of the nineteenth century the changes which have taken place in institutions and in attitudes in even the most backward of the advanced economies is such that the classical type of market economy as described in the foregoing paragraphs is almost unrecognizable. It is a contention of this book that it is precisely because of the changes of institutions and attitudes which have taken place with accelerating speed since the turn of the century that the economic problems of the advanced countries, such as the six we have identified, have arisen. The central question is whether the market economy can continue to operate effectively in the contemporary advanced economies, under the changed circumstances in which it finds itself. It is tempting to conclude that either the changes in institutions and attitudes must be reversed, or else the market economy must fail to fulfil the functions expected of it, functions it performed tolerably well until the turn of the century.

In the nineteenth century, the size of firms was small, and production was concentrated on one product or on a narrow range of related products. Cessation of production by one firm, for whatever reason, would have no more than local repercussions. Today, firms are fewer and larger,[2] and the cessation of production by a large firm has very substantial repercussions, not only on employment directly, but also on employment amongst suppliers. Although there is today a significant proportion of production which is publicly owned in most of the advanced countries, it is from considerations of size rather than from ideology that governments have been increasingly willing to intervene in market processes to protect particular firms from closure, and even to help them secure contracts. In recent years, Lockheed, Chrysler and Rolls Royce all provide examples of private firms whose closure would have had devastating and geographically concentrated employment effects, had there not been government intervention.

The internal organization of the firm has changed with

size; there has been a corresponding change in the motives of those controlling the firm, and therefore in their responses. Ownership has been divorced from control. Shareholders are no longer likely to be active individuals, but financial institutions seeking investment outlets for life assurance funds and workers' pension funds. Galbraith seems to be quite right about the replacement of the entrepreneur by the growth of 'technostructure' in larger firms. (In this connection, figures such as Rowland, Laker and Maxwell seem to be the exception to the rule.) The Austrian observation that all men act as entrepreneurs is scarcely helpful here since the question is: who carries out the function of innovation in the large organization? The answer to this question really depends upon the existence of a theory of socialist or organization behaviour, accepting that the large private corporation is really a socialist institutional form.

Over the last hundred years the institutional characteristics of capital markets in the advanced economies have changed significantly. In the nineteenth century, the capital market brought together the savings of individuals and the borrowings of a multitude of small firms. At the present time, the supply side of the market is dominated by large institutions (life assurance companies and pension funds), through whom the savings of individuals are increasingly channelled. In most countries tax advantages exist for those putting money into pension and life assurance funds. At the same time such large institutions have neither the knowledge nor the willingness to take the risks involved in investing in small firms. As far as the demand for capital is concerned, the large firms, which increasingly dominate the productive sector of the economy, tend to draw upon their own internally generated savings for the greater part of their capital requirements. Inevitably, therefore, there has been an associated change in the climate of risk-taking and risk aversion, and the response of the supply of capital to such things as changes in the rate of interest, changes in the rate of inflation and in the expectation of these changes cannot be assumed to be what it was in the past.[3]

In all of the advanced countries, the government has come

to play a far greater role as a borrower in the capital market. In 1981, borrowing by the federal government absorbed about one-half of all net new saving in the United States. The growth of government borrowing has its counterpart in the fact that there has been a vast expansion in the provision of social security throughout the advanced economies. This might have been expected to diminish the need for saving on the part of individuals, and therefore one should expect to find that the proportion of total household income which is saved has diminished over time. On the other hand, as a result of saving habits throughout the population and the redistribution of income, it may be that the aggregate proportion has not changed significantly. This is an empirical question.

Although the material benefits of economic progress have been eagerly accepted by the population of the advanced countries, the process of economic growth set in motion, directly and indirectly, powerful resistances in the form of the evolution of institutions and attitudes unfavourable to growth. Some of these institutional changes have occurred spontaneously; others have come into existence as the result of legislation. This distinction corresponds to the distinction drawn by Menger between 'organic' and 'pragmatic' phenomena. Amongst the significant organic phenomena are the growth of the influence of trade unions, and the change in the size and nature of productive organizations. The progress of the division of labour and of technology has meant increasing uncertainty and vulnerability for firms: hence the diminished role of the small family firm, and the growth of the multinational corporation, an institutional form particularly well-adapted to cope with change and uncertainty. Although nominally private in its form of ownership, the large corporation partakes of many socialist characteristics.

Three major categories of legislative action relative to growth can be identified in the recent history of the advanced countries. These are regulation, taxation and the establishment of public monopolies. There can be little doubt that in most of the advanced countries the taxation of income and capital gains has taken the edge off the traditional material incentives which formed the basis for the expansion of the market economy. Likewise, the growth of the market economy has increasingly been fettered by government regulation, while protection is accorded to the publicly owned sector.

Let us, first of all, consider the principal spontaneous or organic changes which have taken place in the market economy of the advanced countries. How have they come about? The essence of the market economy is continuing change, both quantitative and qualitative. Change takes place principally through (a) the extension of the division of labour and (b) through cost-cutting competition made possible by technical progress.

Extension of the division of labour

Kuznets has painstakingly assembled estimates of the growth of economic activity in the advanced countries over the past century, classified largely into Keynesian categories. It might prove to be an even more difficult task to assemble quantitative evidence of the progress of the division of labour in the same countries over the same period. A first approximation might be offered by the extension of the list of occupational categories contained in the periodic censuses of population over the period and countries concerned. A further measure might be provided by a series of input–output tables for an individual country, prepared on an identical system of classification of activities. In the early stages of development, the first quadrant of the table would be empty. As functional specialization increased, one would expect to observe that an increasing number of cells in the first quadrant would have non-zero entries. If the input–output tables were spaced out evenly in time, it might even be possible to determine whether the progress of the division of labour had been uneven or monotonic. Associated with this extension of the division of labour, there has been a shift in the composition of household demand and an acceleration in the rate of technical progress. Together these changes have resulted in a marked shift in the composition of output from agriculture and other primary activities towards services, and in the composition of employment from the unskilled to the semi-skilled. So far, although the rate of growth of employment in the manufacturing industry has ceased in most of the advanced countries, there has not yet been an absolute decline in the numbers employed in industry.

It will be realized that Allyn Young attached great importance to the 'search for markets' as a factor determining the speed of progress of the division of labour. When Adam Smith wrote *Wealth of Nations* he envisaged the extension of markets as being a territorial matter, that is, the breakdown of internal barriers to trade within a nation, or the removal of barriers to trade between nations, or thirdly the opening up of new colonies. The eradication of internal barriers to trade was achieved in most of the advanced countries at a comparatively early stage of their development. So far as international trade is concerned, there was a substantial degree of freedom of international trade among the principal advanced countries in the quarter-century leading up to the First World War. Following the Second World War, there followed a further quarter-century which saw substantial multinational reductions of trade restrictions between the industrialized countries, leading effectively to a free trade in industrial products between these countries. More recently, the protectionist tide has begun to flow in the opposite direction, and there are very clear signs that the established principle of free trade has gradually become more eroded. However, there can be little doubt about the association between the liberalization of trade and the historically high rates of growth in the post-war period.

Both Smith and Marx placed great emphasis on the importance of colonies providing opportunities for the continued expansion of the market economy. Again, it can hardly be denied that the 'opening up' of Africa and parts of Asia, which occurred over a comparatively brief time-period by several European powers, did realize substantial economic benefits. Although the distribution of the gains from colonization remains a matter of political dispute, it is remarkable that the withdrawal of European powers from their colonies following the Second World War appears to have had few negative effects on their rate of growth.

The statistics of international trade appear to show that the rate of growth of trade amongst the advanced countries has been much greater than the rate of growth of trade between those countries, on the one hand, and their former colonies, on the other. This lends support to the suggestion that the extension of the range of products, through technical progress, has perhaps taken the place of territorial expansion of markets as the main source of further expansion of the division of labour. A further feature of the post-war extension of the international division of labour has been the fact that, contrary to neo-classical theories of international trade, trade between countries has taken place within the same categories of commodities. The growth of multinational corporations has meant that a manufactured commodity sold in one country may be composed of parts made in many different countries.

This further extension of the division of labour has led to a degree of integration of the economies of the advanced countries which is greater than that assumed by the neo-classical theory of international trade. Amongst other things, it has meant that political intervention in the negotiation of large business contracts has become almost a matter of routine.

Although the expansion of the market economy unleashes forces favourable to change, and thus to growth, it also unleashes countervailing forces which have the opposite effect. For example, it is generally recognized that confidence is one of the most important elements in the business investment decision. Yet not only has the accelerated rate of technical progress increased uncertainty; so, more fundamentally, has the continued extension of the division of labour. This stretched the chain of dependence to an increasing number of links, thus enhancing the uncertainty and vulnerability of any individual decision unit. This uncertainty can be used to explain the sluggish behaviour of investment in the post-war trade cycles in the advanced countries, and it has even been used by Shackle to explain the great depression of the 1930s. It is precisely the effect of uncertainty on the individual business decision which constitutes the only plausible argument in favour of the command economy as a method of organizing economic activity in an advanced society, and it also explains the interventionist tendencies in the direction of so-called indicative planning, which have taken place in some of the advanced countries since the Second World War.

The extension of the division of labour can be seen to have increased the vulnerability of individual industries, regions and even countries as a consequence of specialization. Within each of the advanced countries there are continuing political pressures for the protection of individual industries against the 'threat' that they may be wiped out overnight by foreign competition. In the United States, the phenomenon of one-plant cities, such as Seattle and Detroit, and textile and mining ghost towns are an example of the potential social costs of adjustments which are incurred by the process of specialization when it is carried to extreme lengths. The most startling example of the vulnerability of a community resulting from the extension of the division of labour was the way in which the United Kingdom was threatened by the cutting off of supplies of food and other raw materials in each of the two world wars of this century.

Competition

In the case of the market economy, the benefits of technical progress to a society are realized through the competition among firms in the introduction of cost-cutting and quality-enhancing innovations. Perhaps the most familiar example of this process is the periodic re-tooling of motor-car assembly factories, an event which combines the following phenomena:

1   a substantial additional investment of capital;
2   a substantial substitution of labour per unit of output,
3   the introduction of new technology in the assembly of the finished product;

4　the introduction of improved technology in the product itself.

The combination of each of these four factors is designed to achieve a lowering of unit cost and an improvement in quality sufficient to give a selling advantage over the products of the firm's competitors. Competition between firms in the manufacturing and services sectors of the advanced countries has taken the form of a continuous process of innovation directed at cost reduction, quality improvement or both. This classical view of the nature of competition, laid out clearly by Marx more than a century ago, provides a better understanding of the growth of a market economy than does the neo-classical theory of the market, including the contributions of Robinson and Chamberlin. The weaknesses of the neo-classical approach, notably its assumptions of static technology and product homogeneity, are illustrated by the lack of satisfactory empirical studies carried out in this tradition (with the possible exception of markets in primary commodities), despite many attempts. Although the neo-classical theory is acceptable as a theory of value, it is quite unsatisfactory as a theory of how the market economy grows over time. Empirical evidence in support of the classical theory is to be found in some non-academic studies of the behaviour of individual firms or industries. For example, a recent study of the gradual penetration, and eventual dominance, of the markets for electronic consumer goods in the United States by Japanese manufacturers over a period of twenty years, from 1958, shows that they followed a strategy entirely consistent with the classical theory of competition.[4] Again, one successful multinational company, Black & Decker, has remained a leader in virtually every market segment that it has entered, largely as a result of its strategy of achieving continuous productivity increases through innovations in technology, organization and product quality.

The classical view of the market process, based on competition through innovation, leads to a very different explanation of investment activity than that provided by accelerator theories of the neo-Keynesian type. The latter were used to predict investment activity at an industry level, or even at a national level. They were based broadly on the degree of capacity utilization, and it would be impossible for such theories to account for new investment coexisting with under-utilization of existing capacity. In fact, this is quite a common phenomenon in the modern world, as new technology can make profitable an investment in a new plant in an industry where there is substantial underutilization of existing plant.

Technical progress

Although the classical economists were right to emphasize the role of technical progress in competition, with hindsight it is clear that they, along with most of their neo-classical successors, greatly underestimated the importance of technical progress generally. There can be little doubt that the rate of technical progress has accelerated remarkably in the course of the last hundred years. One indicator of its rate of increase is the number of people who are engaged in scientific and technical occupations. It has been suggested that the majority of scientists and technologists who have ever lived are alive today, nearly all of them in the advanced countries. Nor is technical progress any longer the passive stream of inventions which Adam Smith took it to be. The rate of progress itself can be influenced, at least in some fields, by investment in research and development expenditures. Indeed, so rapid are the developments in some fields that it has been suggested that the further a firm falls behind in its research programme, the more difficult it is for it ultimately to catch up. A further aspect of the phenomenon of accelerated technical progress is the fact that, again in some fields, an innovation may not mean production for sufficiently long to cover quite a short payback period before it is superseded by a further innovation. It is certainly technical progress which is responsible for the situation in the advanced countries today, where there is apparently an excess supply of would-be entrepreneurs (those seeking to turn inventions into innovations) in relation to the supply of capital which is available for such risky or venturesome projects.

Despite the fact that Marx regarded technology, together with ownership of the means of production, as being one of the primary determinants of relationships in a market economy, we still know very little about the social consequences of rapid technological change. However, it may be said that many recent developments in technology are of a nature which have caused decisions on resource allocation to be increasingly removed from the sphere of the market economy and placed under political control. One such development is that of nuclear technology. The question of the safety of nuclear processes is not, as many people believe, a scientific or technical problem, but a social and economic problem, since it supposes that neither war, nor civil disturbances, nor riots, nor criminal activity will increase significantly. In the present condition of the advanced countries, this is a heroic assumption indeed. Since the Industrial Revolution began in the advanced countries, each generation has bequeathed to the next a larger and larger capital stock. However, as a result of the use of nuclear technology in trying to increase the level of material consumption, this may be the first generation for several centuries in the advanced countries to have bequeathed to posterity liabilities which exceed our assets.

A less dramatic illustration of the social consequences of technical progress has been the growth of international standardization amongst the advanced countries. Practices as diverse as accounting, weights and measures, transport, posts and telegraphs, and containerization have all been standardized among the advanced countries and, in some cases, throughout the world. This is a further indication of the cosmopolitanizing tendencies of technical progress operating within a market economy, which was noted both by Adam Smith and by Marx.

In the past, choice of technology has been based on a criterion of profitability, which is equivalent, under certain circumstances, to a maximum-growth criterion. It is possible to envisage the sequence of technologies which have been adopted in the advanced countries as representing a sort of turnpike which has brought us to the position we are in today. Such is the level of material abundance which has been created in the advanced countries that these societies can afford now to adopt technologies which are less efficient but more in line with individual human needs.

In remarking upon the dramatic technical innovations which have been made in the advanced countries, we should not, however, lose sight of the fact that the spectacular progress in material living standards which has been realized in these countries has not been brought about by technology alone, but by technology in combination with the division of labour, competition and the accumulation of capital, which are made possible by the operation of a market economy.[5]

Institutions

Amongst the factors working in favour of change in the advanced countries has been the development of institutions, which are either adapted to change or are directed to promoting change. One such institution is the multinational enterprise, which, in the words of the chairman of one such firm, is specifically organized to adapt to change and to cope with uncertainty, two of the key phenomena of economic activity in the advanced countries of the present day. According to the United Nations Report of 1978, multinational enterprises account for some 20 per cent of the world's output (excluding the centrally planned economies). Their aggregate output is reported to be growing at an annual rate of 10 per cent, which means that their share of total output is likely to go on increasing in the foreseeable future. Multinational enterprises are most active in research-intensive sectors, and their concentration is most marked in primary commodities, branded manufactured goods and skill-intensive services. They have been described as a vehicle for transferring intangible assets across national boundaries, and their existence tends to reverse the traditional assumptions of neo-classical international trade theory. Factors of production controlled by multinational companies may not be mobile between industries within a country (at least not between industries outside the control of the multinational), but they are mobile between countries, within the same sector. Despite outward similarities, the forms of contractual involvement and the nature of the services supplied by the multinational enterprises differs significantly in the last quarter of the twentieth century from those of the late nineteenth century. In particular, one can foresee growing collaboration between multinational enterprises from advanced countries and state-owned companies in developing countries. Greater constraints are likely to be placed upon the operation of multinational enterprises by governments; these productive organizations will, in turn, receive the benefit of operating in a more certain and predictable environment. The successful competitive strategy of Japanese firms operating in overseas markets has already been mentioned. Two other Japanese institutions which facilitate change may be mentioned. First, there are the Zaibatsu, which by operating an internal policy of full employment remove the resistance of their workforce to change. Then there is the Ministry of International Trade and Industry, which provides the institutional framework for the import into Japan of new technology and its implementation in that country. It is not suggested that a successful growth performance in the modern world depends upon other advanced countries adopting Japanese institutions. The Japanese experience does suggest, however, that other countries should have institutions which are capable of performing the same functions as those performed successfully in Japan. The apparent success of the French planning arrangements is an example of different institutional arrangements performing similar functions.

Supply of labour

Perhaps the most important institutional change to have arisen within the market economy in the last century has been the growth of the trade union movement. The trade unions provide an example of an organic response to the system envisaged by Adam Smith, but their development was entirely unforeseen either by Smith or by Marx.

Whether trade unions resulted in despair from uprootedness or simply as a bargaining instrument for better real wages and conditions of work, there can be little doubt of the importance of their influence on the path of development of most of the contemporary advanced countries. Trade unions have been responsible for the development of wage determination through collective bargaining, which at the industry level has some role in conventional theory through the Keynesian labour-supply function. However, collective bargaining at the national level has no place in conventional theory. Much neo-classical literature has devoted itself to investigating the effects of unions upon nominal and real wage rates, both of their own members and of the workforce as a whole. It has been suggested that, up to a certain date, wage claims were based upon the performance of the particular firm in which the claim arose, whereas at a later date claims were made according to the performance of the industry as a whole. Later still, it is said, wage claims have been based upon the performance of the national economy. This historical oversimplification does indicate the tendency for wage expectations to reflect increasingly national rather than local considerations. It is in connection with these national wage rounds that trade unions have been tempted to use their influence at a political level, not only to put through legislation favourable to their own particular short-term interests, but also to attempt to influence aggregate incomes policies. This has happened much more in Europe than in the United States, and it is particularly true of the United Kingdom, Italy and Sweden. Indeed trade union influence has reached the point in the latter three countries where the elected governments find it difficult to legislate without the consent of the unions. However, it is at the level of the plant, or firm, that the unions have exercised perhaps their most decisive influence upon the performance of the advanced economies. Unions have acted as a conservative force to slow down the rate of change by resisting measures to improve productivity and to permit the mobility of labour and the introduction of advanced technology. A variety of restrictive practices have been introduced and accepted under the guise of various propositions such as 'the rate for the job' and 'last in, first out'. The organized trade union movement has directed its influence against such fundamental attitudes and institutions of the market economy as: (a) the competitive interaction of a large number of firms which are price-takers rather than price-makers, (b) innovative entrepreneurship, (c) the acceptance of a high profit rate, (d) the acceptance of the occupational mobility of labour, and (e) the acceptance of an appropriate system of material incentives.

A further major influence upon the supply of labour in the advanced countries has been the dramatic fall in the birth-rate which these countries experienced following (with a time-lag of some thirty years) the beginning of their industrialization. What the precise motivational changes were which caused family sizes to be reduced remains obscure, but that they took place is certain. Although this has resulted in a slower rate of growth of the population, the rate of growth of the labour supply has been increased in some countries and in some periods by an increase in participation rates (primarily of females) and by the immigration of labour.

Turning now to the pragmatic, or legislative, changes which have 'fettered' the growth of the market economy through regulation, taxation or public ownership, we must inquire into the reasons for the hostile attitudes which underlie such legislation. These can be grouped into four categories.

The first of these are the unsettling effects of change, from which protection is sought from the legislature by those affected. Although the material benefits of change have been eagerly accepted by the population of the advanced countries, the disturbance of the settled conditions of life, which is the inescapable price of change, sets in motion powerful political resistances. It is the adjustment forced upon particular industries and particular regions in response to change within the market economy which is the cause of so much social unrest and discontent within the advanced countries. Paradoxically, much of the political resistance is led by socialist parties, so that this movement may be said to be an essentially conservative one in practice, whatever revolutionary ideas it may proclaim.[6]

Although there is no reason in principle why publicly owned enterprises should not be subjected to the same pressures as privately owned enterprises within a market economy, it is significant that, in the UK, most of the industries chosen for nationalization have been those which faced serious problems of adjustment. Sometimes other forms of 'cushioning' against the need for adjustment are found by governments, for example, direct state subsidies to private firms. The critical question is whether the subsidies are directed towards adjustment of the firm or industry in the direction of change, or whether they are directed towards protecting the firm or industry against change. Nearly all of the regional unemployment problems in the advanced countries arise from unsuccessful attempts at resistance to change, frequently encouraged by the governments of those countries.

Secondly, the market economy is, in the words of Mishan, 'uncongenial to the psychic needs of ordinary men'.[7] Some illustration of this proposition is given in the next chapter. Meanwhile, it may be sufficient to note that it is the very rationality of the market system which is resented. The potential reduction of all aspects of human behaviour to material or cash terms is, at best, unheroic and unlovable and, at worst, degrading.[8]

Thirdly, there is the question of inequality. Although it may be argued that the social-class system created by the market economy is less rigid than the class systems of either a feudal or a socialist society, nevertheless it appears to have produced powerful egalitarian responses.

The growth of attitudes favourable to equality, which has been so markedly characteristic of the past fifty years, may be viewed as a reaction to the class system created by the process of industrialization. Although the income inequalities of the nineteenth century might be justified by such arguments as the lifeboat metaphor, or by Keynes's remark about the 'tacit understanding', it is curious why the belief in equality has taken so long to arrive. After all, the universal franchise was accorded in most of the advanced countries by the end of the First World War. The simplest explanation may be that it is only the relatively recent release from material necessity which has meant that there is no longer any apparent justification for sacrifice. From the point of view of the operation of the market economy in the advanced countries, the significant factor about the growth of the ethos of equality has been the strengthening of tendencies towards the narrowing of income differentials. This has prevented the effective operation of the market economy in the labour-market.

Finally, there is uncertainty. As we have observed earlier, the progress of the division of labour means the extension of a longer and more vulnerable chain of interdependence. Since vulnerability makes people uncomfortable, it is understandable that there should be political pressures to diminish uncertainty. This may, in part, account for the strong protectionist pressures now making themselves evident in the advanced countries.

Inflexibility

In the previous section we indicated how some institutions in the advanced countries had altered to facilitate change. However, the great majority of institutions and attitudes have moved in exactly the opposite direction, that is, in the direction of greater inflexibility and rigidity, so that the contemporary environment of institutions and attitudes in the advanced economies is quite different from that presumed to exist by Smith and by Marx.

The changes which we have noted all point in the same direction, towards an increasing resistance to the processes of adjustment upon which the classical theory of economic growth depends. The net result is the increasing inflexibility in the way in which advanced economies of the present day actually operate. This is the principal reason why the problems which we have identified have arisen.

It is ironic that just as the neo-classical theory of value was displacing the classical growth theory as the principal pre-occupation of economists, the conditions for the operation of the market economy began to deteriorate in the most advanced of the then advanced countries, the United Kingdom. And just as the rate of refinement of the theory of value accelerated after the Second World War, so too did the deterioration of the operation of the market economy acceler-ate. For example, in the case of the United Kingdom, one can compare the adjustment which was made in the period 1945–50 with that which took place following the first major increase in the world market price of crude oil in 1973–74. In the former case, the adjustment required was much greater, involving the replacement of capital which was destroyed or worn out during the war, the increase of exports required to earn foreign exchange to pay for wartime debts, the increase of consumption to satisfy private demand, and the increase in public consumption required to satisfy con-temporary social and political aspirations. Yet this adjustment was made relatively smoothly in contrast to the response of the UK economy to the adjustment required following the oil price increase of 1973–74. This suggests that there was a significant deterioration of the adaptability of the UK econ-omy between 1945 and 1975. Subsequently, other of the advanced economies have shown symptoms of the 'English disease', most recently West Germany.

The mobility of factors of production between sectors of an economy in response to changes in demand, resource availability and technology is one of the central features of the growth process. We have already observed how the mobility of the factors of production in the advanced countries has changed remarkably between the nineteenth century and the present day. Other sources of inflexibility include a lack of sharpness in the perception and exploitation of new opportunities, partly as the result of the preference for a quiet life on the part of entrepreneurs, and partly attributable to what Schumpeter called 'the quenching of capitalist motives'.

It must be emphasized that all of these resistances to change are not exogeneous burdens which have been laid upon the market economy, but are constraints which have been generated directly or indirectly by the evolution of the system itself.

7

The Origins of some Contemporary Problems

Slow rate of growth

It should first of all be made clear that for many, if not most, of the advanced countries the rate of growth of their gross domestic product in real terms in the two decades following the Second World War was fast by historical standards. The sense that this rate of growth was too slow may be explained with reference to a faster rate of growth of expectations, and by comparison with the most successful of the advanced economies with whom they were trading. The progressive liberalization of multinational trade which occurred amongst all of the advanced countries following the Second World War, together with an accelerating rate of technical progress, made possible the extension of the international division of labour on a hitherto unprecedented scale. These were the principal factors accounting for the rate of growth of output. However, less obviously, the very success of the system generated increasing restraints and resistances which gradually hindered the flexibility of its own operation.

Since the nature of the growth process is one of adjustment in response to new products, new markets, new technology and new wants, it follows that the proximate cause of too slow a rate of growth is the failure to seize sufficiently strongly these opportunities. Such failure is an entrepreneurial responsibility and may be divided into positive failures and negative failures. Positive failures on the part of entrepreneurs include principally a response to opportunity which is too late or insufficiently strong. For example, the Nora Report showed that a failure to go all the way in introducing new technology may be worse than useless.[1] All the economic costs of re-equipment, redundancy and retraining are incurred, plus the social cost of disturbance. Unless the new cost levels are lowered to those of the firm's principal competitors, the firm will remain at a cost disadvantage. This view is consistent with the classical view of competition as a process of cost-cutting through innovations in organization and technology.

As an example of negative failure on the part of entre-preneurs, one may quote the widespread acceptance of a mass of restrictive practices by managers in British industry over a long period of time in the post-war era.[2] This point raises the question whether entrepreneurial failures should be attributed primarily to an absolute scarcity of entrepreneurial talent, or simply to the existence of an environment unfavour-able to the supply of entrepreneurship. The striking disparity in performance between companies operating in an identical environment suggests the former, though it is also reasonable to suppose that an improvement in the climate would lead to more entrepreneurs being forthcoming. This is really an empirical question concerning the shape of the supply curve of entrepreneurship.

A climate hostile to entrepreneurship has arisen from changing attitudes favouring equality, the growth of trade union influence, government regulation and taxation. Through taxation, changing attitudes have dampened the enthusiasm of entrepreneurs, diminished profits and distorted the structure of incentives. Trade unions have acted to restrict occupational mobility, slow down technical progress and substitute a centrally determined wage bargain for the determination of a set of relative wages by a market system. Finally, the increasing uncertainty and vulnerability arising from the extension of the division of labour may have contributed to the slowing down of the rate of investment in some of the more mature of the advanced economies.

These constraints on the performance of the economy,

growing since the beginning of the century, have accelerated in the last twenty-five years. By 1980, the British economy had reached the point where there were insufficient profits to provide employment for the labour force at non-decreasing real wages. Trade union pressure for higher money wages, unaccompanied by corresponding increases in productivity, but acceded to by government monetary policy, has led inevitably to inflation and unemployment. It has also led to a maldistribution of resources between industries. This has resulted in low productivity in the aggregate, and low profits in the aggregate. This, in turn, has led to a low rate of growth of output per head in the economy as a whole.

Tests of the comparative adaptability among the advanced economies were provided by the 'exogeneous shocks' of the two major oil price increases which took place respectively in 1973–74 and 1979–80. On each occasion the primary effect of the oil price rise on the advanced economies was deflationary in terms of demand and inflationary in terms of costs. On each occasion the advanced countries, individually and collectively, experienced tendencies to a fall in output, an acceleration in the rate of domestic inflation and a sharp deterioration in their balance of payments on current account. It is therefore interesting to compare the speed with which each country was able to restore each of these variables to its normal trend value. It may not be an accident that the most heavily unionized economies were among the least adaptable.

A necessary consequence of the crude-oil price change must be to bring about a transfer of income from the oil-importing countries to the oil-exporting countries. If the inhabitants of the oil-importing countries will not accept lower money wages, then inflation may accelerate to bring real wages down, which it will, provided that the government concerned will accommodate this mechanism with appropriate monetary and fiscal policies. If, on the other hand, governments pursue stricter monetary and fiscal policies, as they did almost uniformly following the second oil price rise, and if some inhabitants successfully resist a reduction in their real wage, then the unemployment of other inhabitants must result. The slower rate of growth of output is brought about because of the fact that, in a modern advanced economy, adjustment to a fall in demand takes place first on quantities and then later on prices. Such a statement can only be justified in aggregate terms: in practice, some industries respond quite differently to others.

Unemployment

Since the demand for labour is a derived demand, it follows that it is affected by factors operating in the product-market as well as in the labour-market. In the previous section, I discussed the influence of factors in the product-market; in this section, I will confine myself to factors operating solely in the labour-market itself.

It is my contention that unemployment in the advanced countries today is primarily the result of the failure of the economies concerned to adjust to change.[3] Thus, at any given period, differences between the unemployment levels of the advanced countries may be explained by the greater flexibility of those economies with the lowest levels of unemployment, namely, Japan, Switzerland and West Germany. Looking at the advanced countries as a whole, the rising levels of unemployment in the decades since the Second World War may be explained by a combination of a faster rate of change of exogenous variables (principally technical progress, internal expectations and the degree of external competition), combined with an increasing resistance to adjustment within the advanced economies themselves. Although the proximate cause of increasing resistance within the labour-market is the increasing inflexibility of market institutions, more important are the underlying changes in attitudes which have brought this inflexibility about. Such attitude changes may be reduced to three: first, the decline of the work ethic; secondly, the fact that gross material deprivation is no longer an alternative to work; thirdly, status and self-respect have come to be measured by money income.

These three changes, in turn, may be reduced to one: that in the supply of labour, as in many other aspects of modern life, the principle of entitlement has replaced the principle of obligation.

The principal inflexibility on the demand side of the labour-market springs from the extension of government control, which occasionally through minimum-wage legislation, but more generally through taxation, has pushed up the fixed cost element of hiring labour to some 15–30 per cent of the nominal wage rate. On the supply side of the labour-market, the major institutional factor is the trade union and nation-wide collective bargaining. But even more important on the supply side are the attitudinal factors. In those countries where unemployment and related social security benefits are significant, people are no longer driven by the alternative of starvation to undertaking menial tasks.[4] As Frank Chappell has noted, people are no longer willing to accept *just any* job: it has to be one which affords them a degree of self-respect. The increasing 'professionalization' of jobs is an illustration of this movement. Similar considerations of status influence the *wage rate* at which people are willing to offer their services, and there is a strong feeling of entitlement to an offer of employment in the same occupation in which the person has initially had employment or training. Finally, there is, of course, territorial immobility: there are very considerable differences between the advanced countries in the willingness of people to move home in search of employment: in some, such as the UK, this reluctance is reinforced by the particular way in which rented accommodation is provided. But it may also be said that the basic reluctance is there: once again, there is a fundamental feeling of entitlement to employment being offered in the existing area of residence *and* in a particular occupation, on terms acceptable to the supplier of labour. Most such examples of inflexibility, which prevent the terms on which labour is offered being matched by the terms on which it is supplied, can be reduced to questions of attitudes; and thus differences in employment between advanced countries, or within one particular country over time, can largely be explained by differences in, or changes in, such attitudes. This 'structural' explanation of unemployment has the advantage that it does not differ from the explanation of unemployment put forward for the developing countries.

It may be suggested, however, that in the case of the advanced countries, an accelerating rate of technical progress must eventually diminish the aggregate demand for labour and lead to a permanent level of involuntary unemployment. This argument is usually illustrated by reference to dramatic examples of substitution of labour by capital in particular industries (for example, the microchip, robot assembly plants). However, a moment's reflection will show that, although technological progress may frequently have brought displacement of labour in individual industries, it cannot lead to an overall decline in the demand for labour in *all* industries, unless one postulates the satiation of consumer wants for material goods and services. The prospect of satiation in the foreseeable future, even in the advanced countries, is slight. However, the foregoing statement must be qualified by the recognition that there has already taken place a perceptible substitution of leisure for work, and that this tendency may be expected to increase. But this problem is no more than a problem of adjustment, to which a flexible economy ought to be able to respond. Indeed, the fall in working hours in the advanced countries in the last eighty years by 25 per cent illustrates that such an adjustment has already been taking place.

However, there is an important adjustment in labour-markets which in theory may not be possible.[5] It is possible that technical progress may operate to increase the demand for skilled labour (using 'skilled' in the widest sense to include managerial and administrative as well as technical skills) and to diminish the demand for unskilled labour. In that event, there may be a physical limit, placed by natural endowments, to the extent to which unskilled may be transformed into skilled labour. In fact, in the foreseeable circumstances of the advanced countries this is unlikely to be a *practical* problem.

It is difficult to see any limit to the demand for, or needs for the provision of, such services as health, education and security, all of which are, or may be, highly intensive in unskilled labour. Thus, once again, we are faced with a problem of adjustment.

In a flexible economy, relative wages should adjust to bring supply and demand into balance in different markets. But in the contemporary advanced economies, such adjustments are inhibited by the operation of increasing examples of inflexibility, some of which we have noted, and in particular by the prevailing ethos of equality, which has replaced, to a large extent, earlier motives behind the supply of labour. The influence of this ethos in the labour-market is that wage differentials outside a narrow band have become unacceptable. If the wage differentials necessary to balance markets should be wider than the 'approved' range, then the consequences are understandable — an excess demand for labour at the highly skilled end of the scale, and an excess supply of labour at the other end. Thus, senior executives are grossly over-worked and suffer from a variety of stresses, whereas there is huge unemployment amongst the unskilled.[6]

Unemployment amongst the unskilled is no longer a serious problem (or it need not be) in a *material sense* for those who are unemployed in the advanced countries. The United Kingdom can afford at present to spend some £10 billion per annum on unemployment benefit, job-creation schemes and related benefits. This is an amount in excess of the annual defence budget. Whether this is a prudent expenditure is another question entirely. The point is that an advanced country can afford to support materially its unemployed workforce. For many of those, particularly the unskilled, unemployment may well be a preferred alternative to a dirty, menial or boring occupation. For others, however, probably the majority, such considerations may be outweighed by a loss of self-respect. These are people for whom the traditional work ethic (the feeling that there is a dignity in work for its own sake regardless of the unpleasantness of the occupation) is important.[7] Sending such people a cheque through the post may satisfy their material needs, but it may, more seriously, destroy their self-respect, because the community is in effect saying that it does not require a contribution from them.

What are the attitudes which underlie the ethos of equality? Adam Smith's pecuniary motive — the desire for material self-improvement — was balanced in his philosophy with the need to enlist the sympathy of the impartial spectator. Until recently, it may be said that this sympathy was conferred on physical labour. As physical labour did violence to human nature, it was clearly a moral good since it fulfilled the ancient Christian principle of obligation.[8] However, the economic progress of advanced countries, driven largely by the pecuniary motive, has swept aside all other motives. Physical work is no longer a necessary sacrifice, because physical work (in the brutal sense) is no longer needed. The dignity of man — his self-respect — is no longer measured by his willingness to undertake physical labour, but by the size of his material income. Even occupational status has become determined by the size of income. In the advanced countries, a pop star or a pimp for the Playboy Club is thought more worthy of respect than a canteen waitress or a parish priest.

If the worth of a person is to be measured by his income, and if it is agreed that all men are of equal (spiritual) worth, then it must follow that all incomes be made equal — or as nearly so as possible. In this way the contemporary attitude of entitlement (in this case a job of a certain status and income) has come to take the place of the ancient principle of obligation.

Inflation

The population of the victorious nations of Western Europe and North America emerged from the Second World War with heightened expectations concerning their material living standards.[9] Being democratic countries, the politicians did not fail to respond to these pressures. Commitments were made to increases in both public and private consumption, which most of these countries, particularly in the context of the huge backlog of capital formation and foreign-exchange repayments necessitated by the war, could not realize from their productive capacity. Thus there arose an excessive consumption in relation to production which has dogged some of the advanced countries, notably the United Kingdom, ever since.[10]

Following the UK devaluation of 1949 the overriding aim of economic policy was to maintain the new currency parity, a policy which was successfully carried out until 1967. Most of the other advanced countries, like the UK, wished to avoid devaluing against the dollar. Thus the other advanced countries had to follow the United States in adopting policies of only limited demand expansion. After the collapse in 1971–73 of the Bretton Woods regime of fixed exchange rates, national governments of the advanced countries felt free to pursue purely domestic objectives. The UK was not alone in boosting domestic demand, a policy which, followed on an international scale, produced soaring commodity prices. In the early 1970s the US government itself was pursuing highly inflationary policies, initially as a result of the Vietnam war. Thus the correct decision to float sterling in 1972 was accompanied by a mistaken indulgence in deficit spending and monetary expansion. Inflation in the advanced economies, which had been held in check throughout the 1950s and 1960s by the need to maintain parity with the dollar, was thus unleashed in the 1970s.

A further stimulus to the rate of inflation was contributed by the fourfold increase in the world-market price of crude oil in the period 1973–74, accommodated by monetary policies in most of the advanced countries. The differential response of the domestic inflation rates in each of the advanced countries to this (and also to the 1979–80 increase) is an instructive measure of the relative capability of each economy for adjustment and thus for growth.

Depletion and pollution

Whereas the first three of our stylized problems are associated with too slow a rate of growth of national output, the problems of depletion and pollution follow from an allegedly too rapid growth of output or, to be more precise, from an allegedly too rapid growth of the industrial part of the total national output. As we shall see, depletion is not an immediate problem so far as material resources are concerned. Whether it might become a problem in the future depends once again on adaptability. If societies are able to adapt to the shortage or even the complete disappearance of one or two primary commodities, then there need be no general problem.

Evidently changes in the social sphere cannot directly affect the availability of natural resources. However, human motives and preferences can determine the rate at which they are depleted, and technical progress influences the costs at which they can be extracted. At any period of time, each society is restricted in its choices by the prevailing supply of natural resources and the state of technology. A hundred years ago there was no general concern about the supply of natural resources to the advanced countries, although there had been some concern earlier in the nineteenth century. Today there is widespread concern, despite the slender empirical evidence of increased scarcity except in the case of one or two specific commodities, such as oil. Since the time of Adam Smith, economists have regarded the progress of human society over time as a race between technical advance, on the one hand, and limited natural resources, on the other. But the importance which they have attached to this problem has fluctuated. The concern which had existed amongst economists in early nineteenth-century Britain evaporated with the arrival from North America of supplies of low-priced corn, made possible by the cultivation of virgin lands and the lowering of transatlantic transport costs.

The issue has once again been brought to public attention by the recent, much publicized suggestions that the world as a whole may be running out of supplies of exhaustible or non-renewable natural resources.[11] Although the depletion of these stocks in a physical sense appears undeniable, most contemporary economists have been inclined to accept the fragmentary empirical evidence available, which suggests that there has not been depletion in the economic sense. Technical change, economies of scale and product-factor substitution have meant that extractive commodities have become *less* scarce in terms of the sacrifices required to obtain them over the past hundred years.[12] The results of nearly all of the empirical studies which have been made support the apparent complacency of economists in the face of the physical depletion of the world's stock of non-renewable resources. For example, Leontief concludes: 'The principal limits to sustained economic growth and accelerated development . . . are political, social, and institutional in character rather than physical.' He continues: 'The problem of the supply of mineral resources for accelerated development is not a problem of absolute scarcity in the present century, but at worst it would probably mean exploiting less productive and more costly deposits of existing minerals, and the intensive exploration of new deposits.'[13]

However, the interpretation of these empirical findings needs to be qualified on at least three grounds. First, continuation of trends observed in the recent past cannot be taken for granted. Secondly, the method of these studies frequently ignores the environmental costs of resource extraction, transport and processing. It is possible that these costs have risen sufficiently fast to offset the decline in market costs of production. Thirdly, there are other externalities which are likewise not considered and which may be of even greater importance.

One such externality which is overlooked by conventional methods of analysis is the political consequence of the expansion of the nuclear energy programme. It is well known that one technological substitute for non-renewable energy is the production of energy through nuclear fission. Quite new risks are associated with the introduction of this technology, namely, the possible failure of emergency cooling systems and the production of plutonium and other long-lived radioactive fission products. To prevent disasters arising from the activities of criminals, psychopaths or fanatics will require what Mishan has described as 'an un-precedented extension of the internal and international security system'. The report of the 1976 Royal Commission, commenting on the 'possible long-term dangers to the fabric and freedom of our society' observed: 'Our consideration of the matter has lead us to conclude that we should not rely for our energy supply on a process which produces such a hazardous substance as plutonium unless there is no reasonable alternative'.[14]

Discontent

Among the more eloquent proponents of the argument that the psychological consequences of economic growth in the advanced countries have, on balance, been adverse is Mishan. It is his argument that the progress of the past century has produced a civilization which is 'uncongenial to the psychic needs of ordinary men' and which, at the same time, has 'undermined the social attitudes and institutions which invest all free industrialised societies with stability and cohesion'.[15] In other words, it is alleged that the psychological benefits of higher material living standards are insubstantial and are out-weighed by the psychological costs: specifically, the material progress experienced by citizens of the advanced countries has lead to a tendency towards emotional enfeeblement and to the creation of social discontents, which, in turn, tend toward the establishment of political dictatorship. I will now consider these arguments a little more carefully; first of all, I will discuss the discontents arising in the sphere of consumption, then in the sphere of production, and then I will examine to what extent they may be said to be undermining the social order.

In the sphere of consumption, rising real incomes accompanied by technological progress have lead, in Mishan's view, to a 'feverish search for novelty and excitement which is fostered and met by commercial interests'. However, since it is the emotional, intangible and non-rational factors which are the most important ingredients in the lives of ordinary people, technical novelty can offer no long-term satisfaction, but must result in either emotional enfeeblement or frustration and even despair. A further source of frustration in the sphere of consumption has been brought about by a relative fall in the real cost of travel, with the consequent congestion not only of city centres but, more importantly, of tourist sites in the advanced countries. Congestion is a source of stress in daily life, and the inability to enjoy in tranquillity outstanding sights of natural beauty is a source of frustration. A third source of unease which afflicts the citizen in his capacity as consumer arises directly from the rate of change of organization and of personnel. This undermines the comfort which is drawn from the continuation of the familiar, as well as the sense of belonging.

In the sphere of production, it has been generally accepted that the tendency towards large-scale firms using ever more capital-intensive technology is increasingly dissatisfying from the point of view of the workers: in short, their degree of alienation is aggravated. Indeed, Schumpeter has gone so far as to argue that participation of workers in any productive organization cannot be based on an impersonal legal contract alone: some degree of loyalty to the organization on the part of the worker is an essential ingredient. It is axiomatic that this degree of loyalty depends on a strong personal component. There are many examples which bear this out. Perhaps the most obvious is the agricultural industry, where, despite lower wages and generally less favourable conditions of work than in manufacturing, relations between worker and non-absentee farmer are less hostile than in manufacturing, because of the element of personal contact. Even within the manufacturing industry, observers of small firms have remarked that the degree of hostility exhibited by workers is generally less than in larger, more modern plants in the same industry,

where wages and working conditions are apparently, objec-
tively speaking, better.

It is equally clear that the progress of the division of labour
tends to accentuate social-class divisions, thus fostering pride
and envy, which cannot but help undermine the social order.
The kind of education provided by the state in most of the
advanced countries in the last hundred years – essentially an
education with a technical and vocational rather than a liberal
bias – has simply aggravated the problem, because it has
served largely as a screening process, further sharpening class
divisions.

One further source of discontent that may be noted is
associated with the territorial mobility of labour which has
been such a marked characteristic of growth in the advanced
countries. In particular, the mobility of labour associated
with the Empire in the nineteenth century led to numbers
of people being uprooted from their native countries and
transported as a workforce to other countries. V. S. Naipaul
has remarked that people transported in this way, and their
descendants, find difficulty in fulfilling themselves outside
their native land. Such rootlessness may explain the discontent, for example, of the urban Irish in the USA, or the
disproportionate number of trade union activists in England
with Irish or Scottish backgrounds. It may be that rootlessness accounts for the greater discontent – despite higher real
wages – in urban than in rural society. Perhaps also the myths
of working-class exploitation may be better explained by the
loss of such intangibles, including status, than by material loss.

It may not be unreasonable to suggest that the factors
which we have outlined above have given rise to frustration
and emotional enfeeblement which may, in turn, be in part
responsible for the indicators of social decay which we noticed
in chapter 1. They may also be, again at least in part, responsible for the undermining of the social order.

There are, however, two much more fundamental difficulties with the process of economic growth in the advanced
countries. First, the distribution of rewards has taken place
on a morally arbitrary basis. The success of the system in

producing economic growth has been due to the distributional principle of productivity: talent has been rewarded. But talent is morally neutral. Moral neutrality is responsible for the separation of knowledge from truth and for the separation of motive from action. Secondly, the extension of the division of labour has resulted in a compartmentalization of life which is destructive of human nature. The division of labour has destroyed what Weil calls 'the spiritual quality' of physical labour. Such compartmentalization of human life is illustrated by the way in which the practice of religion in the advanced countries was at first segregated into a function to be fulfilled in one part of the week, and then was extinguished altogether, although it is still practised as a social function by some members of the middle classes. Education has come to be interpreted as the transmission of technical knowledge rather than the transmission of values. Indeed, it might not be too much of an exaggeration to say that in the advanced countries applied science has come to be universally accepted in the twentieth century as a substitute for conventional religion. Conventional ecclesiastical authority has not merely been questioned, but has long since been disregarded, whereas the authority of practitioners of science, especially of applied science, has been totally unquestioned. So overwhelmed are the inhabitants of the advanced countries by the achievements of technology that the family man washing his car on a Sunday morning has become the contemporary analogue of the practice of worshipping the golden calf. Those who cannot find in technology an adequate substitute for conventional religious belief take their comfort in miscellaneous cults and horoscopes.

It is likely that it is these more fundamental considerations which led earlier writers such as Huxley, Weil and Orwell to perceive an association between economic growth, emotional impoverishment and political dictatorship.

Extension of government control

Adam Smith's institutional prescription for sustained economic growth included the withdrawal of government control over economic activity other than in the provision of the framework of law and order, certain limited public works and defence. In contrast, the variety and depth of government control in the modern advanced economy has become so pervasive as to defy classification. Indeed, it is easier to identify those controls which a government does not possess in a modern advanced economy; these principally would be the power of the direction of labour and the allocation of consumer goods by rationing. However, in principle, existing taxes and subsidies could be so arranged as to provide incentives sufficiently powerful that such decrees would scarcely be necessary. Indeed, Schumpeter pointed out that the controls which existed in post-war Britain were actually more extensive than those which would have been required to operate a market socialist system (although not quite so extensive as would be required to operate a command economy). Although the degree of acceptable government control appears to have proceeded further in some advanced countries (United Kingdom, Italy, Sweden) than in others (Switzerland, West Germany, United States), it does seem as if the rate of extension of control is accelerated by major upheavals such as wars and periods of major depression and/or inflation.

Since the Second World War government control has been extended in the following major areas: stabilization policies, income redistribution, price regulation, regulation of labour and money markets, social security legislation and, most recently, highly detailed regulations for the operation of particular industries, with particular reference to consumer protection, environmental protection, and health and safety at work. In addition, the range of goods to be provided to the citizen by the state, whether free or paid for like the Post Office, has been expanded rapidly in the post-war period, and there seems to be no reason to doubt that the range could be extended indefinitely. Other than the acceptability of the tax burden and 'the priorities of government expenditure', there seems to be no limit perceived to this process, at least in some advanced countries.

Those who view the extension of government control with great misgiving are quick to point out that the particular justification which is used in each case may not matter very much. They point to the 'unintended consequences of human action' which they illustrate with reference to the history of the federal regulatory agencies in the United States, and argue that the most significant aspect is the expansion of political control over the individual citizen, which follows from the expansion of state control of economic activity.

Reasons for the extension of state control

For Schumpeter the explanation was quite simple; for him the central economic and political issue of our time was the transition from capitalism to socialism, and this process, generated by the nature of the market economy itself, could be measured by the degree of the extension of state control. Amongst the proximate causes which are responsible for this movement are the political pressures which arise in a democratic society in favour of government intervention to secure benefits for particular groups in society, or to protect other groups from the consequences of change. In some countries, one class of pressures is stronger than the others. For example, in the United States, congressional 'log-rolling' is a long-standing and successful procedure. On the other hand, in the United Kingdom, government intervention has been on the side of 'protecting' income and employment groups threatened by change.[16] Both Schumpeter and Hayek believe that political pressures generated in a democratic system will ultimately impose constraints which make a market economy unworkable. To this end, Hayek has advocated the adoption of a significant change in political institutions in advanced countries: namely that one of the two chambers of the legislature should be elected for a period of fifteen years so that its members would be immune from short-term political pressures.

A more pragmatic view is offered by Mishan, who puts forward four reasons for the extension of state control. First, the existence of a progressive income tax combined with a growing economy; secondly, the presence of egalitarian sentiments; third, the nature, rate of increase and diffusion of technology (motor cars, package flights, nuclear energy) justifies the assumption of increasingly totalitarian powers by the state. Finally, social disintegration requires government intervention to the point of dictatorship: 'an instinct for survival is propelling the Western democracies along the road to the totalitarian state'. What Mishan evidently has in mind is that the fourth category of causes is the erosion of status based on tradition, and status becomes dependent only on money and position in the occupational hierarchy. The legitimacy of social institutions then becomes increasingly under assault and only the extension of the power of the state and the contraction of personal freedom can prevent the disintegration of the social order.

Whatever the validity of these arguments as explanations of the extension of state control, one explanation which can be ruled out is the ideological one. Those political forces which believe in government intervention as an end in itself have had insignificant political influence in the advanced countries, and their force now seems to be spent. Thus the extension of state control has not been based on any conscious ideological decision. We have seen the conservative Republican administration of Mr Nixon in the United States imposing wage and price guidelines, and preventing major companies such as Lockheed and Chrysler from becoming bankrupt. Likewise the Heath government in Britain intervened to prevent the bankruptcy of Rolls Royce and Upper Clyde Shipbuilders. Even the later Thatcher government, supposedly more ideologically opposed to government intervention than its Conservative predecessor, has given thousands of millions of pounds of subsidies to ailing companies, both privately and publicly owned, such as British Leyland, British Steel and ICL.

Consequences of the expansion of state control
The first and most obvious consequence is the proliferation of the bureaucracy which can be measured by the number of

employees of central and local government. Despite this huge expansion in employment, and therefore presumably in the volume of services provided, popular expectations about government have been disappointed to an even more marked degree than is the case of popular expectations concerning the rise in the material standard of living. This, in turn, has led to the legitimacy of democratic government being questioned. Perhaps the only way for democratic governments to recover their legitimacy is for them to confine themselves to those functions which are (a) necessary and (b) can be performed effectively.[17]

Why has the government failed to match the expectations which were created in the post-war world? We cannot answer this question, because we have no general theory concerning the behaviour of bureaucratic organizations. In this connection, bureaucratic organizations not only include central and local governments, but also public corporations and large private corporations, and even non-profit-making bodies like trade unions and universities. All have in common the fact that their affairs are not guided by market forces. In the advanced economies, the area of economic activity controlled by the market has continuously diminished as the area controlled by bureaucracy or organization has expanded. Even such a long-standing critic of the market economy as Galbraith has confessed that the relatively poor performance of the contemporary advanced economies may well be due primarily to the predominance of the organizational over the market form of economic control. The chief characteristics of the bureaucracy which are conducive to poor performance are inflexibility, senility and 'the perpetuation of mediocrity'. The bureaucratic system, by severely punishing errors, but seldom rewarding success, is therefore highly inflexible.[18]

Some writers have been more alarmed by the political, than by the economic, consequences of state control. Friedman, for example, believes the market economy is a necessary, though not a sufficient, condition for political freedom. He writes: 'I know of no example in time or place of a society that has been marked by a large measure of political freedom, that has not also used something comparable to a free market to organise the greater part of its economic activity.' This empirical proposition is backed up by the theory that the market economy promotes economic freedom because it separates economic and political power, and thus enables the one to offset the other. Since the greatest threat to political freedom is the concentration of power, the scope of government must be limited and such government power as exists must be dispersed, that is, devolved to the lowest level and scattered, as in Switzerland. Such a point of view is not really very different in principle from that of Adam Smith in his conception of natural liberty. This view of the political process, with collectivism, or the corporate state, being placed at the opposite end of the political spectrum from individual liberty, was expressed most forcefully by Hayek in *The Road to Serfdom* (published in 1944). At that time his identification of the socialist tendencies within the British Labour Party with the socialist tendencies of Nazism seemed hysterical, but at the present time it seems less far removed from reality. It is significant that many of those who feel that the advanced countries are heading for more authoritarian forms of government do not trouble to distinguish whether there will be an authoritarianism of the 'Left' or of the 'Right'. Both Friedman and Hayek are followers of the nineteenth-century liberal traditions, of which one of the key assumptions is the belief that each man is the best judge of his own interests. In this tradition, too, decisions are the outcome of individual choices. In the advanced economies of the present day, most of the major decisions which are taken are not made in the area of life controlled by the market, but rather in the sphere of politics. That is in the sphere in which the exercise of choice is not individual but collective. Such a choice cannot effectively be exercised without a broad degree of consensus on the part of the electorate.

8

Prospects for the Future of the Advanced Economies

This chapter looks at what may happen in the advanced countries over the next twenty to thirty years with particular reference to the ways in which changes in tastes and technology will influence economic organization and institutional arrangements. This chapter examines the most likely outcomes, while the last chapter examines policy implications.

It should be made clear at the outset that I reject any idea of historical determinism or inevitability. Like Schumpeter, I only hope to discern tendencies which may be diverted, stopped in their tracks or even reversed. There is the further consideration of different outcomes in different countries; because of diverse historical, geographical and cultural circumstances, Sweden may follow a different path from France. The ability to achieve different outcomes arises from unequal abilities to call on the reserves of tradition, the machinery of administration, or the sheer good fortune of political life. One major reason why I reject inevitability is the capacity of groups of human beings (as well as individuals) to learn from their past mistakes. To what extent they do so is another matter, and this may be yet a further source of international differences.

In the last hundred years, there is considerable evidence of convergence among the industrialized countries in terms of technology, tastes and therefore of attitudes and institutions. Although, as we shall see, it may be that this pattern of convergence will reverse itself, I shall only try to deal with those

tendencies which are common to all of the advanced countries. In this chapter four stylized alternative sets of institutional arrangements are discussed. They are:

1   the restoration of the market economy to something like its traditional form;
2   the mixed economy or social market economy or social democracy;
3   the command economy;
4   alternative arrangements.

Paradise regained: the market economy restored

In 1949 Joseph Schumpeter clearly set out his view of likely changes in the economic organization of the United Kingdom and the United States.[1] In particular, he concentrated on the question of the likelihood and probable rate of change in economic institutions in these countries from capitalist to socialist forms. He predicted that, despite temporary setbacks, there would be a continuing, gradual but perceptible movement in both institutions and attitudes in the socialist direction. Although he was careful not to commit himself to any grand prophecies, it is clear that, reading between the lines of his paper, he expected that the ultimate outcome of this process would most likely be some form of politically authoritarian government operating a virtually command economy. There are at least two reasons for taking this prediction seriously. First, it is perfectly clear that he himself found such a transition extremely disagreeable. Secondly, reading his writings with the benefit of thirty years' hindsight, one cannot but be impressed by the accuracy of his predictions. In 1949 it must have seemed inconceivable to anyone else that a future British Conservative government would be nationalizing major private companies, or that a Republican administration in the United States would introduce wage and price guidelines. Schumpeter himself would have been the first to emphasize that because he has been right so far, this does not mean to say that such tendencies will continue or that his ultimate forebodings will be realized. It does, however, suggest that we should pay careful attention to what he has to say.

He predicted that there would be periodic right-wing governments which would attempt to turn the clock back in the direction of a traditional private-enterprise free-market economy. He did, however, warn that the reversals in institutional arrangements and in attitudes which would be required to restore the market economy to its previous state of unburdened operation would prove to be more than would be politically acceptable. Evidence in favour of the correctness of this prediction is provided by the fate of the 1979 Conservative government in the United Kingdom. Prior to and following its election, the government stated quite plainly its objective of removing the main burdens on the operation of the market economy so that inflation could be brought under control, while taxation was simultaneously reduced. After three years in office, the government has failed to achieve any of these stated objectives.[2] Apart from removing controls on incomes and on international capital movements, it has not attempted any major institutional changes. Such successes which it has had in lowering the expectations of wage claimants may have been brought about by the effects on unemployment of a major recession and may not survive a subsequent expansion. The particularly important objective of a reduction in government expenditure has not been achieved. This government expenditure protects a bastion of privileged employees who enjoy security of tenure, pensions indexed against inflation and relatively high real incomes, all of which are denied to their counterparts in the market-economy sector. A further and substantial part of government expenditure is devoted to subsidizing loss-making productive enterprises in the nationalized-industry sector. The present government has also been markedly reluctant to weaken by legislation the bargaining power of the trade unions.[3] However, whether because of the current level of unemployment or for other reasons, there does seem to have been a growing acceptance of the principle of occupational mobility on the

part of the unions. In the context of adaptability as a response
to change, the single most important restrictive practice of the
unions hitherto has been their refusal to accept job mobility
within plants, and the reluctance to accept retraining between
plants.

The mixed economy

As we have seen, the environment of institutions and attitudes
within which the market economy operates in the advanced
countries of the present day is so far removed from the
environment of the late nineteenth century as to constitute
a different form of economic and political organization. It is
true that in the great majority of these countries the ownership of the greater part of the productive capital is still
nominally 'private'. But the divorce of ownership from
control has robbed private property of much of its meaning,
and in any case the Marxist criterion of ownership, which is
supposed to mark the transition from 'capitalism' to socialism,
does not appear to be very helpful.

Whatever the degree of public ownership in each country,
all of the advanced countries operating a market economy
are burdened with such constraints that it has been aptly
described as an attempt to operate the capitalist engine in
the labour interest. This stage can be described as a mixed
economy, democratic socialism or social democracy. It is
sufficiently far removed from the traditional or pure market
economy that most forms of neo-classical economic analysis
have only limited applicability.

Schumpeter did not believe that social democracy would
have a long life. The reason was that the groups which made
up such a political entity would lack sufficient self-discipline
to allow the system to work properly. In his view, social
democracy would prove an unstable half-way house between
capitalism and socialism, and the frustrations which it would
generate would tend to lead further in the direction of socialism rather than to bring about a reversion towards the

traditional market economy. For Schumpeter, the critical watershed on the transition to socialism would occur with what he called the 'socialisation of the labour market', what we would nowadays call a permanent statutory incomes policy.

Since the Second World War successive governments in the United Kingdom have dabbled with temporary 'incomes policies', with an invariable lack of success. Not only have such policies proved to be ineffective, they have also proved to be extremely unpopular. It is difficult to see how even a fairly authoritarian government in an advanced country such as the UK could easily overcome the unpopularity of a permanent statutory incomes policy, let alone a social democratic government. Even in the unlikely event that the set of relative wages could be agreed for all occupations throughout the country by some objective measure, it seems most unlikely that they would be generally accepted subjectively as being 'fair'. This is because each individual places a different valuation on the worth of his own labour services from the valuation which is placed on them by his neighbour.

Hayek has another explanation for the unpopularity of permanent incomes policies:

> Once it becomes increasingly true and is generally recognised that the true position of the individual is determined not by individual forces . . . as a result of competition . . . but by the deliberate decision of authority, the attitude of the people towards their position in the social order necessarily changes . . . dissatisfaction of everybody with his lot will inevitably grow with the consciousness that it is the result of deliberate human decision.[4]

And again:

> a fixed rule like that of equality [of income] might be acquiesced in, and so might chance or an external necessity, but that a handful of human beings could weigh everybody in the balance and give more to one and less to another at

their sole pleasure and judgement, would not be borne
unless from persons believed to be more than men, and
backed by supernatural terrors.[5]

Again, even if a particular set of relative wages could be
agreed, changes in circumstances arising from changes in
technology, resource availability, tastes, etc., would mean the
need for a continuing revision of the set of wage relativities –
thus losing the notional consensus. Otherwise, a growing
discrepancy would arise between the chosen relativity and
the efficient set of wages. An illustration of this phenomenon
is the recent breakdown of Norwegian incomes policy as
wage rises granted to workers on the North Sea oil fields
spread throughout the economy. It is tempting to argue that
if a permanent statutory incomes policy cannot work in
Norway, it cannot work in any democratic country, since
Norway has the advantage of being an exceptionally homogeneous society with a continuing consensus on the broad
lines of economic and social policy.

Now that Keynesian economic policy has been abandoned,
it is difficult to see any theoretical underpinning for a 'mixed
economy' in the contemporary circumstances. On the other
hand, it must be said that, despite evident dissatisfaction with
the major political parties, there are no signs whatsoever that
voters would opt for an extreme solution. At the present
time, the advanced economies are full of institutionally
sanctioned inefficiency, while rents and windfall profits
accrue in a random way, unintentionally influenced by
government action. A very much more marked deterioration
in economic performance would have to be forthcoming
before the electorate would be driven to one political extreme
or the other. Much more likely to emerge is what might be
described as an authoritarian government of the centre. The
distinction between public and private ownership of large-
scale enterprises will have been further blurred, and government intervention in all details of the economy will be tacitly
accepted. Thus the principles of a command economy will
operate alongside those of a market economy. Such a govern-

ment will no doubt periodically attempt to determine wage rates. It is one of the ironies of the situation that the principal institutional obstacle to the imposition of a permanent incomes policy remains the trade unions. They are blocking the road to socialism.

If the market economy is, as we have argued, characterized by a continuing change in institutions and attitudes, political institutions cannot be expected to be exempt from this process. There is no reason why the existing social order should be sacroscanct. Indeed, democratic societies depend for their cohesiveness and stability on certain institutions and attitudes which may have been undermined by the process of substantial economic growth. Lord Salisbury is said to have once described democracy as 'putting the cat in charge of the cream jug'; he presumably meant that the workability of the type of democratic political system shared by all of the advanced countries depends on the existence of a common degree of self-denial on the part of individuals and groups in those societies. Yet it can hardly be doubted that in the course of the past century, self-denial and self-discipline have been replaced steadily by self-indulgence and self-advertisement as the prevailing attitudes amongst the majority of people in these societies. Without self-discipline, a democratic socialist economy cannot work, since the external disciplines *either* of the traditional market economy *or* of the command economy are lacking. At the same time, the overwhelming majority of people in the advanced countries are deeply attached to the principle of political democracy and would accept its disappearance only with the greatest reluctance.

The command economy

If we accept the proposition that a permanent statutory incomes policy is not consistent with a democratic society, and if we further agree that a command economy cannot be operated without direct control of the labour-market, which implies not only statutory wage control but also direction of labour, then a command economy cannot be compatible with a democratic political system. To this it might be objected that the UK economy during the Second World War operated as a command economy, and might therefore serve as a model of how a command economy could work within the democratic political system of an advanced economy. This comparison is vitiated by two vital considerations. First, at the time of the Second World War there was a sense of national emergency which made people quite willing to forgo temporarily their usual democratic rights. Thus, a fundamental change of attitudes took place. Secondly, people were also willing to forgo their accustomed standard of living, again temporarily. In the period since the Second World War, the range and sophistication of consumer goods and services has grown beyond all recognition, and it is precisely in this area that the command economy appears least able to perform satisfactorily.

A political dictatorship might come about in an advanced country through one or more of three possible routes.

1   If economic decline or stagnation continues, people may accept a dictatorship in the hope of getting the 'engine' of economic growth to run again.
2   Internal social upheavals, arising indirectly from the various discontents of economic life and expressed through vandalism, racial and class violence, etc., might lead to the 'necessity' for the imposition of martial law.
3   A third possible reason for a dictatorship would be the proliferation of technologically dangerous substances, so that the security of society as a whole could only be maintained by a ruthless vigilance on the part of the authorities.

It may be argued that the extension of the division of labour in the advanced countries has now reached the point that the individual has but a slight chance of opting out of a thoroughly interdependent system, without an unacceptable fall in his material standard of living. The strength of the chain of interdependence is only as great as the strength of its weakest link, and if one or more links should prove to be, or appear to be, fragile, then the appeal of an authoritarian collectivist solution may be overwhelming. People may wish for the certainty, order and a sense of cohesion and continuity which an authoritarian collectivist society is well placed to provide. Such a society might also provide an explicit principle of social obligation.

Whatever its merits in these terms, the historical evidence suggests that the economic counterpart of political dictatorship, that is, the command economy, simply does not work. No socialist society (with the possible exception of East Germany) has ever produced a satisfactory economic system.[6] Experience of such economies suggests that they can deliver a small range of priority goods (military, space), but have greater difficulty in delivering the quality and diversity of modern industrial and consumer goods. The flaw in the system may not be the informational one claimed by the critics of collectivism who wrote in the 1930s. Indeed, developments in information processing may well make it possible for the centre to acquire the kind of information which is necessary for static resource-allocation directives. It is much more difficult to envisage a command economy being able to orchestrate change satisfactorily. The public benefit which is derived from the existence of a competitive market economy, as Adam Smith was among the first to realize, arises from the greater diversity of thought and decision and thus the greater chances of innovation and development. In the market process, individuals perceive opportunities which are thrown up by change and act thereupon, sometimes prudently, at other times imprudently. It is not the static allocative role assigned to the market by neo-classical theory which the command economy cannot replicate: it is the dynamic adjustment role assigned to the market by the classical tradition.

Just as the market economy produces forces which worked slowly but surely to undermine its own institutional arrangements and the attitudes prerequisite to its operation, it is possible that similar forces are moving to undermine the institutions of the socialist command economies. It would, however, be interesting to have an analysis of what these forces were, and how the interaction of motives, changing tastes and technology with the institutions of a command economy takes place. Marx's failure to write about the political economy of socialism might perhaps be attributed to his tendency to think of people as being a race of one-dimensional men. Although Adam Smith thought of the pecuniary motive as being the overriding one in the market economy, he did not make it the exclusive one in human society.

Reversing the division of labour

Steady-state growth theory perpetuates the idea of economic growth as being one-dimensional, with unchanging forms of input, including technical progress. Classical growth theory, on the other hand, sees growth as a multidimensional process of continuing change, in which a central feature is the continuing extension of the division of labour, that is, of the exchange or market economy. As the division of labour proceeds, however, its costs increase, its benefits become less important and the *form* of technological progress changes, bringing with it changes in institutions and attitudes, and thus changes in the nature of the growth process itself.

The principal sources of cost increases brought about by the extension of the division of labour are twofold. First, the nature of the division of labour implies an increasing number of intermediaries as the division of labour is extended. As the price of labour rises, with increasing prosperity, the transaction costs involved at every stage of intermediation increasingly become a disproportionate part of the total cost of production. A familiar example is the gap between the price of food in supermarkets and farm-gate prices. Secondly, the ever-extending chain of interdependence, which arises from specialization, increases uncertainty, since the chain is only as strong as its weakest link. There are also important non-economic costs of the extension of the division of labour, for example, social costs such as alienation and job search, retraining and unemployment costs. On the other hand, as the result of the diminishing urgency of wants in advanced economies through time, also arising from increased prosperity, the need for income to be earned through the supply of labour to the market economy becomes less and less. Citizens of advanced economies may prefer to take their higher real incomes increasingly in the form of leisure, so that the supply curve of labour to the market economy may have a backward-bending shape. Leisure need not take the form of idleness nor of culture nor of sport, but it may be devoted to own-account work. The growth of a 'home' economy is also being assisted by current developments in technology.

The combined effects of new forms of technology with the costs and benefits which we have outlined in the last paragraph, means the slowing down, if not bringing to a halt, of the expansion of the division of labour which has for so long been the hallmark of economic growth in the advanced countries. This, in turn, has profound implications for attitudes and institutions in the advanced economies of the future.

Technological progress in the advanced countries today is not only accelerating in total, but the new *forms* of technology which are becoming available will have a marked influence on the future course of events in these countries. The two most important changes occur in the combined field of computer and communications technology and, secondly, in the forms of energy production. In the future, the latter will be based less upon non-renewable sources and more upon renewable sources. The consequences of each of these changes in technology is to exert a powerful decentralizing influence on the process of production. The fact that both changes are, by accident, coming about together will only reinforce the power of this tendency. New forms of technology have other interesting characteristics, such as requirement for higher skills in the co-operating labour and lower energy inputs. Technological efficiency will no longer require large 'runs' of a small range of standardized goods. The working conditions associated with this technology will no longer be as boring, repetitive, dirty, dangerous or as noisy as in the immediate past.

All these new forms will enhance existing areas of production; others will represent what may seem like completely new departures: developments in bio-technology and the exploitation of outer space and the oceans. However, these more spectacular forms of technological progress are likely to have less immediate influence on attitudes and institutions than the two decentralizing forms of technology we have just noted.

They are decentralizing because they permit the wider dispersal of at least a part of the working population, both through cheaper and improved forms of communication and through the availability of local energy sources. Although these developments, by themselves, do not directly affect the degree of the division of labour, they make possible a remarkable extension of the home economy at the expense of the market economy, a potential which the preferences of individuals are likely to realize.

The shrinking of the market economy and the development of the home economy have a number of important implications. First, there will be a remarkable increase in liberalization, that is in the degree of freedom of the individual concerning the disposition of his labour. In order to survive, it will no longer be necessary for the individual to supply all his labour to the market. He will therefore have control over the terms and conditions of much of his own labour. It allows the individual to opt out of political as well as economic forms of organization. Secondly, it suggests that classical forms of socialism are much less likely to be realized, since all of them depend upon a high degree of interdepence, that is, a high degree of division of labour within the society. In this respect, socialism is no different from an advanced market economy. Thirdly, it implies de-urbanization.

Fourthly, it implies a greater stability for the family unit, as the home economy may involve all of the family in co-operation in the sphere of work production. This, in turn, can have a favourable effect on youth unemployment, but more importantly it provides the unity of labour which is so important for psychological health, and of which the division of labour is so destructive. Greater family unity and less territorial mobility means, in turn, greater community stability.

However, greater community stability may be attained at the expense of new forms of political rivalries. Although developments in information processing and in energy are likely to have the liberalizing effects I have indicated, other technological forms are likely to increase the importance of government. It seems likely therefore that there will be political rivalry between government and large corporations (whether privately or publicly owned), on the one hand, and small to medium-sized firms, the home economy and perhaps the black economy, on the other. The bureaucracy and the large corporations will represent pressures for security, order and no change, whereas the other sectors of society will represent the interests of freedom and flexibility in the widest senses of those words.

If this perspective is correct, then economic growth in the advanced economies in the nineteenth and twentieth centuries, which was carried out under the strict regime imposed by the interdependence necessary for the exchange economy to function properly, will be seen as a turnpike, at the end of which family units will revert to a degree of independence which they formerly possessed, but which was sacrificed to gain the advantages of higher productivity obtainable through the division of labour. In principle, therefore, we should expect to find that institutional forms could evolve which will make possible for the vast majority of the population the realization of the traditional aspirations of Western civilization. Not only will they be freed from material poverty, but they will also be freed from the constraints of organization required to overcome that poverty. Whether this dramatic potential will be realized is, of course, another question.

Conclusions

One conclusion which is supported by the historical evidence is that the command economy does not work in advanced societies. No socialist society (with the possible exception of East Germany) has ever produced a satisfactory economic system. At a local level, none of the nineteenth or twentieth-century experiments in socialist communities can be said to have worked satisfactorily. Frequently, institutions and attitudes in socialist systems are designed so that incentives either do not work at all or work in antisocial directions. A more fundamental difficulty with socialism is the failure to satisfy the basic human 'need' for ownership of the means of production with which one works.

Of course, economic security, rather than economic growth, may well be the priority of the citizens of the advanced countries of the future. A vote for tranquillity may turn out to be a vote of socialism or at least for some other form of collective authoritarianism. Perhaps a plurality of institutional arrangements is the most plausible outcome of the present circumstances in the advanced countries. Some people will prefer to enjoy the relatively high wages associated with employment in a large multinational corporation, others the security of employment available in the public sector, still others the satisfaction of running their own firm, still others again the satisfaction of belonging to a worker-controlled firm, etc. The questions are whether all these forms can survive in competition with each other, and whether market forces will not, unless checked, cause one form to swallow up all or most of the others. Whatever happens, it does seems as if advanced economies will, to a greater degree than in the past, use political means to try to achieve economic and social objectives. There is a collective learning process and a consequent collective decision-making process. Amongst the propositions which have painfully been learned is that social problems may prove to be more intractable than physical problems. Indeed, if one of the major problems of advanced societies is loneliness, it seems unlikely that this can be solved by any social policy.

All economists in the classical tradition from Adam Smith to Schumpeter have greatly underestimated the consequence of technological progress: not only for the growth of output but also for changes in institutions and attitudes. Foreseeable forms of technological progress may be used as a powerful weapon against the bureaucracy. By making very large numbers of administrative tasks redundant, they will create the opportunity for reductions in employment in the public sector. After existing forms of technology have released citizens of the advanced economies from the thraldom of material poverty, some future forms of technology can release the individual from the thraldom of society, at least in part. At the same time, other forms of technology are 'shrinking' the world, and fewer and fewer people in any country will be able to escape such public 'bads' as noise, pollution and radiation.

In the last section, we referred to a sort of turnpike theorem of technology and society. Starting from the pre-industrial period, today's advanced societies have organized themselves by means of the division of labour principle in such a way as to realize the very large productivity potential of technology, accompanied by specialization. After a point far along the turnpike generating new technology, a level of technology will have been developed sufficiently advanced to permit a swift adaptation to the desired technological end points. The whole movement will thus have permitted the realization of very large productivity increases, without the four principal evils of the market economy: change, alienation, inequality and uncertainty.

9

A Note on Method

The purpose of this chapter is not to review the many recent and distinguished contributions to the debate on methodology in economics and the social sciences. Its purpose is rather to reiterate a number of simple propositions, germane to the purpose of this book, which are often unknown to students and overlooked by their teachers.

In earlier chapters of this book I have argued that neo-classical and Keynesian methods of research and of theorizing in economics are too narrow and that, as a result, contemporary economic analysis has become unduly restricted in its scope to the point where it is unable to offer satisfactory explanations of many issues of current concern.

I do not assert that conventional methods of analysis are wrong: rather, that they can be appropriately applied only to a limited range of questions, few of them of general interest. This is because the questions of general interest in the advanced countries of the present day – as well as in the underdeveloped countries – contain dimensions of human behaviour outside the scope of economics as conventionally defined. Consequently, professional economists today are increasingly in the position of remaining silent, in a professional capacity, on the major policy issues of the day, and their professional contributions to the major debates are confined to a narrow area and are necessarily of limited value. Instead, in their scholarly work, professional economists are forced to look for problems which, although difficult from an intellectual

standpoint, are in substance trivial, since these are the only
kinds of problems to which conventional methods of analysis
can usefully be applied. One of the principal objectives of
this book is to persuade the reader that mainstream economics
should be rescued from this narrow channel of thinking. In
this chapter, I shall not only show the weaknesses of conventional methods of analysis, but I shall also try to suggest what
positive elements of procedural criteria should take their
place.

False notions of scientific method

One of the implicit beliefs of conventional economic analysis
is that the methods of the natural sciences are the only ones
which, when applied in economics, can claim to be 'scientific'.
It is important to recall that there are at least three major
respects in which the natural sciences and the social sciences
differ fundamentally. First of all, there is the well-known
difficulty of controlled experiment in the social sciences.
Secondly, there is the fact that in the social sciences the parameters of the system being studied are continuously changing.
Finally, and perhaps most importantly, there is the consideration that the principal agents in the economic or social
system are not inanimate objects, but human beings who may
be supposed to act in a purposeful manner. Because it is more
difficult to establish a body of organized knowledge in the
social sciences, this does not mean that procedures for tackling
these questions, which are difficult from the procedures
employed in the natural sciences, are thereby any the less
scientific.[1]

The careless application of methods drawn from the natural
sciences to economics has led to the adoption of methods of
analysis in conventional usage which are quite clearly unscientific. Many years ago Morgenstern wrote a book about
the inaccuracy of economic observations, and yet the National
Income Accounts for the United Kingdom still print estimates
of national income and its components in at least six digits,

despite the fact that the error of estimate is admitted to be in excess of 1 per cent. In the field of economic development, there are serious difficulties involved in measuring adequately inputs of labour, to say nothing of capital; the necessary qualifications are seldom stated in the literature. As scientists, we should properly have doubts about the measurability of such apparently quantifiable and all too frequently quantified variables.

A futher example of unscientific behaviour which manifests itself in conventional methods of economic analysis is the use of quantitative methods in cases where these are clearly inappropriate. For example, in the application of time-series analysis to economic phenomena few economists pay very much attention to the limitations which are imposed upon procedure by the assumptions of statistical theory. In the same field of analysis, it is frequently overlooked that 'no statistical procedure can distinguish contingent from causal relations', and that 'different years have their personalities' (Phelps Brown). Again, in the field of econometrics, serious conceptual problems are raised by modelling *ex ante* relationships with *ex post* data, and are invariably ignored in practice. However, it is probably true to suppose that the disappointing nature of the results so far obtained from the application of econometric methods has sprung not so much from the failure to observe strictly the assumptions required by statistical theory but, rather, from the weakness of the theoretical economic relationships which are specified.[2]

A further example of a false understanding of what constitutes scientific procedure in economics concerns the proposition that a hypothesis should be judged purely on the success of its ability to predict. Although this proposition continued to be debated among economists long after it had been discredited in the philosophy of the natural sciences,[3] it is important to understand that its appropriateness in economics has to be judged on different grounds from its appropriateness to the natural sciences. For one thing, the proposition evidently overlooks the difference between prediction in circumstances where events can be controlled

and prediction in the social world of uncontrolled phenomena.
As Schumpeter says:

> it is as unreasonable to expect the economist to forecast
> correctly what will actually happen as it would be to
> expect a doctor to prognosticate when his patient will be
> the victim of a road accident, and how this will effect the
> state of his health.

Criteria for scientific procedures in economics

From the remarks in the previous section it will be clear that
the proposition (implicit or explicit) that the methods appropriate to the natural sciences are also appropriate for appli-
cations in the social sciences is itself unscientific. What, then,
is 'science' so far as economics is concerned? It cannot be
stressed too strongly that 'science' is simply organized knowledge. As Machlup has pointed out, there is a very wide range
of methods in economics that are perfectly acceptable from a
scientific point of view: 'Historical records, fertile intuition,
speculative interpretation, logical deduction, inductive generalisation, heuristic fiction, observation and experimentation,
are all, individually or jointly, equally acceptable'.
  Schumpeter provides another example of methodological
tolerance. In his very first published article he made a plea
for the use of mathematical methods in economic theory.
Two months before his death, he delivered a paper pleading
for the use of the historical method in business-cycle research.
There was no contradiction between these two points of view
because, as he said, 'when at last will the day come when all
will realise that the ocean of facts has innumerable different
aspects which call for innumerable methods of approach?'
Elsewhere, Schumpeter complains that the social sciences
suffer in their contemporary practice from two ills:

1 'that almost childish narrow-mindedness which regards
   its own method of work as the only possible one';

2   'the complete lack of even elementary knowledge of all
    branches of learning outside one's own'.

The latter point is strongly echoed by other Austrians, notably
Von Mises, Hayek and Machlup. In this connection, Hayek
writes:

> Nobody can be a great economist who is only an economist,
> and I am even tempted to add that the economist who is
> only an economist is likely to become a nuisance if not a
> positive danger.[4]

This recognition of the importance of 'non-economic' social
facts, categories and theories in the analysis of specific economic problems is one to which Katouzian also attaches great
importance, commenting that the economist should 'always
maintain the history of relevant ideas and events as a back-
ground to the study'.[5]

The same writer makes an entirely different, but equally
important, point when he states his criterion for the selection
of topics for economic research. According to him, we should
'place a higher priority on the understanding and solution of
important and real economic problems in contrast to minute
puzzles'.[6]

Granted that this is an acceptable criterion for preparing
the agenda for economic research, what are the criteria by
which we might judge acceptable from unacceptable methods?
In order to answer this question, we should perhaps begin
with the proposition that most economists can recognize a
good piece of work in economics when they read it, even
though it might be extremely difficult for them to define the
criteria by which they arrive at such a classification. Despite
the well-publicized disagreements of economists, if the
profession were asked to draw up a list of the ten most
distinguished economists of all time, it is probable that the
same five or six names would appear on 90 per cent of all
lists. We can agree, for example, that Adam Smith, Marx and
Keynes are great economists, and that Galbraith is not. It is
much more difficult to say *why* Adam Smith, Marx and

Keynes should be classified as great economists. The fact that we cannot do this does not make them any the less great. It simply illustrates the difficulty of procedure in the social sciences. It is this phenomenon which perhaps caused Hayek to observe that we should not suppose that we can always state or describe the rules which govern our actions and perceptions.

Pursuing this line of thought, it may be helpful to draw a distinction between the work of a pure scholar, who in the extreme case may be little more than a taxonomist, and the creative economist. One recalls Leontief's metaphor of the ice-breaker, in which the imaginative and intuitive leap of judgement is performed by one kind of economist (the creative kind), whereas the tidying-up operation is performed by the other kind (the scholar). On this same theme, Phelps Brown quotes Darwin:

> Many men who are very clever — much cleverer than discoverers — never originate anything. As far as I can conjecture, the art consists of habitually searching for causes or meanings of everything which occurs. This implies sharp observation and requires as much knowledge as possible of the subject investigated.[7]

The last sentence of this extract recalls the passage from Mill on Smith which was quoted at the beginning of this book (p. 4). It is clear that the criteria which are implied in these two passages for the appropriate procedure for creative economists are very different from the criteria which are applied to the work of a pure scholar. One does not ask if Smith, Keynes or Marx were good at formulating testable propositions or verifying the inferences therefore. Indeed, the greatest works of these writers are openly admitted to be confused and inconsistent from a theoretical standpoint.

The fact is that the great economists belong to the category of creative rather than scholarly writers and that their importance is due to the presence in their work of qualities of vision or imagination. The truth is that in the present climate of

thinking about economic method the importance of imagination or intuition or of vision is almost entirely overlooked.
This is despite the fact that Leontief has written that 'intuitive
conjecture . . . after all . . . is the ultimate source of all analytical insight'.[8] It is indeed commonplace that the starting-
point in much inquiry – not only in economics but in all
fields – is frequently the concern on the part of the investi-
gator for a particular goal. The second stage in the inquiry is
usually intuition, and then investigation of the facts follows.
But the facts are usually selected to fit the intuition. To take
an example from the field of economics, it is well known that
all of Marx's essential ideas are contained in the *Communist
Manifesto* of 1848. His further twenty years of work were
devoted to attempting to substantiate these ideas. And Marx,
surely rightly, should receive the credit for the correctness of
his vision of the passing of the capitalist system, even though
he was wrong about the manner of its passing and quite
confused about value theory. Again, is not Myint's interpretation of Adam Smith's theory of the market simply a difference of *vision* as compared to the orthodox neo-classical
interpretation?

To take yet a further example on the theme of the importance of the imagination in economics, who would deny that
the creative imaginations of such writers as Huxley and Orwell
are not as successful in forecasting key features of the socio-
economic system forty or fifty years ahead as are the more
orthodox approaches of Herman Kahn, to say nothing of
mathematical growth models? This parallel between the
methods used in creative writing and the role of imagination
in economics may not be too far-fetched. In his analysis of
the methods adopted by Adam Smith, Reisman concludes
that partly because of his conviction that science appeals to
the senses and partly because of his tendency to relate beauty
to order, Smith 'came close to identifying truth with beauty,
and scientific method with aesthetics'.[9]

Returning from the lofty heights of imagination to the
more pedestrian criteria to be adopted by scholars, there are
a number of positive suggestions which can be made, despite

the apparent licence offered by proponents of methodological tolerance. One such criterion in choosing method is the suitability of the method to the topic. For example, it is inappropriate, and therefore unscientific, to use value theory for the analysis of problems of growth and development.[10]

A further criterion of acceptable procedure in economic analysis concerns the writer's ability to distinguish between statements of fact and statements of value. In this connection the point should be made that it does not seem reasonable to accept the view implicit in conventional procedure that one value judgement should be assigned no more weight than that of another. More weight should be attached to the opinions of those who speak on the basis of accumulated experience, rather than to the opinions of those who come to a topic with no particular experience at all.

A further guideline for worthwhile economic analysis is that some attempt should be made to appeal to empirical or historical evidence, even if the outcome is not conclusive. This point is related to the earlier remarks about the importance of an economist being aware of cognate disciplines in the social sciences.

On forecasting, perhaps we should be content, with John Stuart Mill, that a vague proposition, however derived, may be 'insufficient for prediction', but 'valuable for guidance', or with Schumpeter's statement 'I do not pretend to prophesy: I merely recognise the facts and point out the tendencies which the facts indicate.'[11]

Another element which is desirable in a good piece of work is a logical consistency both within and between the propositions being used. As we have seen, however, consistency is a virtue which may be outweighed by other virtues. Finally, there is one negative criterion about which it is possible to be quite conclusive. Dogmatism is an inadmissible procedure in economics, as in any other branch of science. For example the statement of Howard and King, interpreting Marx, that 'ruling ideas are nothing more than the ideal expression of the dominant material relationship' implies that these ideas may be dismissed without being subject to logical or empirical examination. Such a proposition is exactly analogous to the statement that Einstein's ideas can be disregarded because he was Jewish. The use of such *ad hominem* arguments by contemporary economists has unfortunately not died out.[12] We should also take comfort from the thought that progress is possible in economics. Schumpeter was surely right to say that Walras's 'Theory of General Equilibrium' represents a culmination of the development of value theory in the neo-classical tradition. The overwhelming majority of economists would agree that this step represented a distinct forward movement over the incomplete cost of production theories of value, on the one hand, and the purely subjective theories of value, on the other, which preceded Walras's synthesis.

Agenda for teaching and research

It is most likely that within the wider boundary of economics as advocated in this book, no hard or settled conclusions can be reached. One of the major differences with conventional methods is that we recognize this explicitly.[13] The question may then be asked: what contribution can the economist make to the discussion of major issues of public policy?

The answer surely is that economists, by contending with each other according to the guidelines outlined above, should be able to raise the level of public debate about contemporary issues of policy. Such an apparently modest objective is one which would have commended itself to John Stuart Mill, who regarded the elucidation of policy matters as being the chief end of economics. All economists must be aware of the abysmal level of public debate on economic-policy issues concerning the contemporary British economy.[14] There is therefore scope for improvement.

What about 'pure' research? Those who have carried out applied research projects will recognize that the terms of reference of commissioned research are frequently designed to fit existing quantitative methods of research and tend to gloss over what are often the more important aspects of the problem because they are non-quantifiable. But pure research projects, too, are frequently commissioned to fit existing data. What is needed are funds for survey work. But to what phenomena would such research surveys be directed? Who will finance them? Some economists argue that to confine research to observed behaviour is futile. According to this view, programmes of research must deal with underlying motivations.

A further addition to the agenda of important research in political economy is a theory of economic behaviour in the public, non-market sector. In this connection some further words of Hayek's are wroth quoting.

> If social phenomena showed no order except insofar as they were consciously designed, there would indeed be no room for a theory of economic science in society; there would be, as is often argued, only problems of psychology. It is only insofar as some sort of order arises as a result of individual action, but without being designed by any individual, that a problem is raised which demands a theoretical explanation.[15]

10

Conclusions

This chapter concerns some normative aspects of economic policy in the advanced countries in the near future. The first part of the chapter deals with general and longer-term issues, and the second part deals with more immediate and specific problems.

If there is a general objective for the future of the advanced economies it must be to devise a technology and a set of institutions which will make it possible for the whole population of these countries to realize the traditional aspirations of Western civilization. The prosperity of the advanced countries already permits a wider range of choice for their populations than was ever previously possible. This prosperity is dependent upon a particular technology, combined with a set of institutions and attitudes. In the future, when material needs in the advanced countries are less pressing, it will be possible to choose alternative technologies and alternative institutional arrangements, together with their concomitant sets of attitudes, which although being less efficient in the production of material goods and services, may nevertheless be more emotionally satisfying.

It may be objected that the advanced countries are characterized by the absence of any consensus — any set of shared values about economic and social objectives: in short, that a common set of values no longer exists amongst the citizens of these countries. If this is the case, then the need for pluralist societies must be frankly recognized. But if these societies are to have any minimum degree of cohesion, then there must be some sort of co-ordinating mechanism for economic activity, and there must be some common principle, or principles, of social obligation.

The future of democracy

Some institutions and technologies will evolve spontaneously: there is very little we can say about them, except to try to predict their development. Others, however, will be the outcome of collective choice. In the circumstances of a collective choice, what solutions to the problems of the advanced countries over the next ten to twenty years can be commended? This choice must be made within the framework of a number of foreseeable tendences:

1　the form, and rate of change, of technology;
2　the diminishing urgency of wants: the greater scope for leisure and own-account work;
3　the necessity of social cohesion;
4　the importance of preserving political democracy.

Given the diminishing urgency of wants, it would seem that economic growth will no longer have the priority that it once had in the advanced countries. It seems more likely to come below economic security and the control of social tensions in the politician's ranking of priorities. Although it is on economic growth that this book concentrates, I have tried to bear these other objectives in mind. The recommendations which are advanced in this chapter are explicitly founded upon the assumption that the population of the advanced countries will prefer to preserve a pluralistic society with a representative government and political institutions characterized by the diffusion of power. Although the precise forms of political institutions may differ from one advanced country to another, and some are undergoing change, nevertheless the institutions of government and their method of operation are broadly similar among such countries. What is meant by representative government is well understood, and the distinction between democracy and dictatorship cannot be disguised.

It may be that in the perspective of history this preference will be seen to be no more than an expression of passing nineteenth-century romanticism. However, the history of the twentieth century suggests that dictatorial forms of government in advanced countries perform very much worse from the standpoint of personal liberty as well as from the standpoint of economic performance and social tensions. Since the advanced countries have provided adequate levels of private and public consumption for their citizens, personal liberty must still be regarded as a major priority. However, it does seem that, in order to survive politically, democratic institutions in the advanced countries may have to become more authoritarian than they have been in the recent past. Ultimately, the viability of democracy depends on the political maturity of the citizenry: they must be willing to accept responsibility, they must be capable of learning from experience, and they must be able to practise the minimum degrees of self-discipline and self-denial.

It may be argued that all this is a pipe-dream and that the realities of democratic politics will lead, via log-rolling, pork-barrelling and 'goal-diversion', to the general interest being submerged in a welter of vested special interests, among which those of the bureaucracy may predominate. To the extent that this is true, then it is one reason why the governments of advanced countries may have to become authoritarian in order to assert the primacy of the general interest. These governments need not be less democratic in the crude sense, but they may become less sensitive to the pressures of minority interest groups. Not only may government in the advanced countries have to become more authoritarian; in order to satisfy the demand for economic security, it may have to become more interventionist. Can democracy survive in any form in the advanced countries?

One does not have to accept all of the arguments of Veblen and Hirsch to realize that, if the many were to aspire to enjoy the extravagant life-style of the few, (a) this would place impossible demands on the economy for decades to come and (b) not much increase in satisfaction would result. It is possible, therefore, that inequality will once again come to be accepted, as it was implicitly in the past, if the few were seen to be providing some essential service to the many, such as making a distinct contribution to raising further their absolute living standards. But this is unlikely. As Adam Smith observed, property excites envy, and the acceleration of technical progress is likely to mean the continuous disturbance of the social order, provoking change and reinforcing the belief in social engineering. This seems the more likely outcome.

If this view is correct, then the most prudent course for the leadership of advanced societies to adopt, so far as life-style is concerned, is one of conspicuous frugality. It is not suggested by this phrase that they should adopt a sackcloth-and-ashes attitude to life, nor even that they should cease to enjoy the good things of life. Many despots have followed a life-style of exemplary frugality. Those who are influential in setting trends should demonstrate by their behaviour that ostentatious and extravagant consumption is unfashionable or in bad taste. For example, it is quite unnecessary that a technically satisfactory motor car should be changed every two years; if the fashion were established for a change not more frequently than once every five years, it would release resources for more important needs rather than for inessential wants. This change of attitude is not something which can be legislated for: it can only be achieved by precept. To what extent pop stars and footballers are amenable to persuasion by the political leadership remains to be seen. There is no doubt that an appeal to a new set of values based upon modest consumption levels would have considerable attraction for those who are seeking leadership and not finding satisfaction in utilitarian materialist life-styles. Such a set of values, if it were widely adopted, would make a positive contribution to the success of a range of alternative policies within the range of possible institutions foreseeable in the next ten to twenty years. The resources thus released, which otherwise would have been devoted to unnecessary private consumption, would be available for investment and/or transfers abroad and/or such labour-intensive areas of collective consumption as health, education and defence (both internal and external).

What institutional arrangements, then, are capable of promoting economic growth while preserving democracy and maintaining economic security, without increasing social tensions? Plurality of institutions is one answer. The co-existence of large commercial, industrial and administrative corporations offering security of employment and freedom from responsibility with smaller units of production, owner-managed or worker-controlled, where those occupied accept lower real incomes in return for a desired share of responsibility.

The organization of the economy

What should the state's policy on intervention and control of the macro-economic processes be? First, there should be state ownership of all large corporations. There are several reasons for this. There is the argument advanced by Walras that profits are composed largely of rents, and that the benefit should therefore accrue to the community as a whole. In an equality-conscious age, where technological change and large size bring political influence and windfall profits, large concen-trations of power are increasingly unacceptable. But those who are familiar with the behaviour of existing publicly-owned corporations in advanced countries may find this proposal an alarming one, because of the practice of such corporations to put the interests of their staff – especially their senior staff – ahead of the interest of their customers. It is important to understand, however, that this practice arises not because the enterprise in question is publicly owned, but because it is a monopoly protected by the state. Accord-ingly, such an arrangement as that proposed would be desirable only if it were to be combined with the organizational prin-ciple of the market economy. This principle should be applied irrespective of whether there is public or private ownership of large corporations. The principle must be that the government should intervene to ensure that a market mechanism operates in accordance with the classical principles of competition: in short, it should be the function of the government to ensure that in every sector of economic activity there should exist sufficient diversity of thought and decision that innovation is encouraged and change is accepted. Government intervention should be actively, principally and continuously directed to the operation of this principle.

The changes which are involved in implementing such a proposal may not be as great as they might at first sight appear. Because of their size the US, UK, France, Germany and Italy are atypical of advanced countries. The great majority of those countries − indeed of all countries − are small and therefore have open economies. Consequently, to the extent that they operate a broadly free trade policy then they are, to that extent, operating a market economy. In the case of the larger countries, prices can be determined internally on the basis of the world market price for the corresponding commodity. Where this is apparently impossible, in the case of a natural monopoly such as the railway or the telephone system, there must be government regulation of price, calculated on proper economic (not accounting or political) bases.

Of course, many monopolies are not as natural as they appear. In the case of both the railways and the telephone system, the possibility exists for either complete regional decentralization (as is proposed for the United States telephone system) or the periodic auctioning of licences or both (as is the case with the United Kingdom commercial television system). Whichever way monopolies are treated, and the second is on the whole to be preferred, the remuneration of the senior management of publicly owned corporations should be statutorily related to the performance of their enterprise.

Alongside large and medium-sized production units one should expect to find spontaneous development of very much smaller units, giving opportunities for self-employment, co-operative ownership or part-time employment. Many of these already exist, and the growth of the black economy and own-account working indicate their organic origins. These developments indicate a tendency for labour to hire capital, rather than the reverse, and there is every reason to suppose that this tendency will increase. We should also expect to find an increasing proportion of the workforce who not only have several different occupations during their working life but also may have more than one occupation at any given time. These sort of developments go a long way towards diminishing the alienation which arises from the extreme division of labour.

The importance of adaptability

It is implicit in what has been said so far that a sustained rate of growth of output per head both of private and collective consumption will continue to be a primary objective of economic policy in all the advanced countries for at least the next twenty years. This is the reason why institutions must be adapted to make changes acceptable, that is, why the distortions in the operation of the competitive process must be minimized. Whatever institutional forms are selected, it is important that adaptability should be built into them, so that when the opportunity for change arises in the quality or in the quantity of the goods and services they provide, they may be able to adjust to this, and not just simply linger on, providing a comfortable living for their employees without a commensurate service being provided to the community.

A major role for government in the promotion of change is that it should take responsibility for supporting adjustments to change and disarming resistance to change. If, for example, the state were to take from trade unions their role of providing economic security, whether through a tax credit or other minimum fixed-income scheme, or through an employment-guarantee scheme, then the role of the unions as one of the principal institutions resisting change would lose much of its justification. It is quite consistent with the objective of economic growth that the state should undertake to provide some employment at all times for its citizens (economic security); it is wholly inimical to economic growth when the state (or any other organization such as a trade union) seeks to maintain some individuals in particular employments.

In the United Kingdom resistance to the relinquishment of particular employment has recently been overcome by the device of redundancy payments, the incidence of which in practice seemed to bear little relation to considerations either of equity or efficiency. No doubt there will always be disputes about the gains and losses arising from change, just as there are continuing disputes about the distribution of income. Nevertheless, the general principle to be achieved is one of realizing collective purposes using a quasi-competitive or quasi-market mechanism as an instrument of control. Specifically, in the case of occupational redeployment, it is evident that new institutional arrangements are required to operate on the supply side of the labour-market. Clearly, the traditional mechanism of each man fending for himself has broken down in large numbers of cases (particularly where there are heavy regional concentrations of unemployment in specific industries). Not surprisingly, this has been associated with intensive hostility to change of any kind. Specifically, what is required is automatic retraining in transferable skills for all who become unemployed, accompanied by the elimination of barriers to entry to occupations following retraining. At the same time, governments must provide economic security: that is, they must always be willing to offer employment of some kind on reasonable terms.

Given the diminishing urgency of wants, it may be asked why one should opt for a market economy at all. The answer is that although the need for material goods may have diminished, the need for health, education and other services is a long way from being satisfied. Experience suggests that the government cannot provide these services efficiently: *why* it cannot provide them efficiently must await an analysis of the non-market sector of the economy.

The pecuniary motive as an acceptable driving force in

society must, however, be balanced by a complementary principle of social obligation. If this does not happen and if unrestrained selfishness, coupled with immoderate expectations, becomes socially acceptable, then democratic societies can hardly be expected to survive. If the forces for change which are unleashed by the market economy are unaccompanied by any principles of social obligation, then Nazi Germany and Soviet Russia provide examples of the possible consequences. In the contemporary world, Iran provides an example of the kind of forces which rush into the moral vacuum which is created when the market economy is unleashed upon a traditional society. Saudi Arabia, on the other hand, shows that the consequences of even the most crude forms of materialism can be contained, where there is present a corresponding principle of social obligation, in this case the code of behaviour required by Islam.

Advanced countries have two major and related problems. Because they are democracies, collective choice must be the result of learning by doing. Societies as a whole must experience for themselves the consequences of erroneous policies before being diverted from them. For example, it has taken the citizens of the United Kingdom more than thirty years to learn the lesson of the inefficiency of public-sector monopolies. It is not a lesson that could be learned merely by being taught. This means that change in a democracy is an extremely slow and wasteful process. It is rather like trying to have a supertanker change course. There is also the danger that some political experiments, such as electing a dictatorship, may be irreversible. This is analogous to an error in navigation which drives the supertanker on to the rocks.

A second major burden on all advanced economies is the bureaucracy. The administrative costs of the government in the United Kingdom are put at some £10 billion. This does not include the costs of compliance. In the phrase of Bacon and Eltis, there are too few producers. There are precedents in history for societies which have disappeared under the weight of their bureaucracy, an organic growth which has always proved remarkably resistant to dislodgement.

We turn now to a consideration of some possible solutions to the six stylized problems facing the advanced countries.

The rate of growth

Few of the advanced countries in the post-war period have achieved rates of growth of output which are satisfactory by their own standards. In those countries where Keynesian thinking dominated economic-policy discussions, growth policy was considered conterminous with the controlled expansion of aggregate demand. The view that private investment was largely demand determined, as opposed to the neo-classical view that investment was based upon profits (expected or past), was extremely influential in the post-war period. The expansion of domestic aggregate monetary demand was taken to be a sufficient condition for economic growth, and little thought was given to the question of how such an expansion of demand might be reflected in increases in prices as opposed to increases in output. The United Kingdom experiments in indicative planning were based upon theories of demand-determined growth. These experiments proved to be a failure, and Austrian critics have claimed that this failure was predictable, due to the inevitable imperfections of knowledge and uncertainty concerning the future. Indeed, they have argued that the increasing burdens of inflation and taxation produced by monetary and fiscal policies have only aggravated uncertainty, and therefore have discouraged business investment.

Such criticisms of indicative planning, however, cannot so easily be reconciled with the apparent success of indicative planning in France and Japan. It may be argued that government intervention in an attempt to promote economic growth in these countries was more successful because it concentrated on those factors which would be recognized by classical theory as being essential elements in the process of economic growth. First, co-operation between government and particular firms in these countries reduced uncertainty for the firms concerned.

Secondly, intervention was, and is, designed to promote acceptance of change and adjustment to change on the part of the firms. Governments in both countries actively support cost-reducing innovations in production and in marketing.

Of course other advanced countries have enjoyed comparatively successful rates of growth without the type of indicative planning arrangements which have prevailed in France. The form of the institutions themselves is not important. What is important is the way in which they function; in particular, the way in which they bear upon the capacity of the particular economic system to innovate and to respond favourably to external and internal pressures for change.

Unemployment

The ultimate justification for Keynesian policies was the attainment of full employment. But only a few years after President Nixon had declared that 'we are all Keynesians now', the then Prime Minister James Callaghan of the United Kingdom explicitly renounced the fundamental tenet of the Keynesian faith when he said to the Labour Party Conference in September 1976: 'we cannot spend our way out of a recession'. This point of view has implicitly been adopted by the governments of the seven major industrialized countries in their response to the oil price rises in 1979–80. They responded unanimously with restrictive monetary and fiscal policies.

Why were Keynesian policies abandoned? Overlooking the explicitly short-term nature of Keynes's analysis, the crude belief had been adopted in post-war policy-making circles in many of the advanced countries that full employment could be maintained in the long run by the simple device of expanding aggregate monetary demand. The observed coexistence of rising rates of inflation with rising rates of unemployment was simply incompatible with this belief, and the traditional view has been restored, namely, that in the long run the level of employment and its rate of growth are a function of real and not of monetary factors. If the real factors determining the level of employment in the economy are favourable, then the stimulus of aggregate monetary demand is unnecessary. If these real factors are unfavourable, then the stimulus of aggregate monetary demand, although providing a temporary palliative in the short run, will have no significant effect in the long run other than to increase the rate of inflation.

What are these real factors determining the rate of growth of employment in the modern advanced economy? They are the same factors which govern the rate of growth of output in the economy, with the addition of these special features which operate specifically to determine the flexibility or otherwise of labour-markets, that is, the capacity to respond to change. In the post-war period in the United Kingdom little attention was given to the fact that even in the 1930s unemployment was heavily concentrated in particular industries, occupations and regions of the country. Post-war UK government policies did not therefore encourage mobility of labour, either occupationally or territorially, and countervailing influences have been strong. It is only within the last few years that constraints on the adjustment of the labour-market to change have been recognized as the major factor determining the long-run level of employment. Thus, the appropriate policies have yet to be tried. These policies should be founded on the principle that, by appropriate measures of compensation and security of income, the government should support adjustment and disarm resistance to change.

When these principles are propounded, they are sometimes met with the suggestion that there are only a limited number of employment opportunities. Of course, it all depends on the terms and conditions of employment, but technical progress in the form of 'information products' and such services as education, health and defence together provide an almost unlimited reservoir of potential job opportunities in any advanced country. This is to say nothing of the opportunities for self-employment and own-account employment.

At the present time the expansion of employment in the services sector is inhibited by the presence of powerful white-collar trade unions. Were it not for their obstruction, redundant or retired unskilled workers could become social workers or paramedical workers. Higher up the skill scale there are possibilities for parateaching personnel and lower down the skill scale for paradefence personnel. Housewives or others tied to households can become excellent home helps, looking after elderly neighbours. These are all indications that long-term unemployment is largely a question of restrictions on the labour supply side of the market, many of which can in principle be removed. Mobility between occupations can actively be encouraged by the government. Where this is impossible, appropriate subsidies may be used to balance demand and supply for particular occupations.

Inflation

The traditional measure for the control of inflation is the adoption of a restrictive monetary policy.[1] In Schumpeter's words, 'it . . . was to apply to a world in which everything was entirely flexible, and which was not afraid of what I may term remedial recession. In such a world, an increase in interest rates was supposed to reduce the volume of operations, money wages and employment.' He continued: 'surely these effects would not materialise today, and if they did, they would immediately provoke government action to neutralise them. In other words, credit restrictions would at present achieve little beyond increasing the difficulties of business.' These words have a particular poignancy at the present time. Although they were true for the 1960s and 1970s, governments since 1980 in the major advanced countries have preferred to accept rising unemployment than to adopt easy monetary policies. The question which remains to be answered is whether these governments will survive the political pressures which are thereby generated, and which might yet force them to change course.

The second traditional way of controlling inflation is by means of increasing taxation. Increased taxes on consumption would be good Keynesianism, but it is not particularly popular politically. If corporation tax and the higher range of income taxes increased, then the effects upon inflationary pressures are likely to be small and might even be negative. This is because, if investment is to continue and firms are denied resort to profits or savings, they would have to turn to borrowing from the banks in order to make up for the decrease in the available non-inflationary means of finance. Alternatively, a decrease in the rate of investment would decrease inflationary pressures for the moment but would increase them in the long term.

The third traditional remedy consists of direct controls. These measures are popular with the bureaucracy and the trade unions, since these give them a political advantage in their battle with the business class. Price control is a major step forward towards a planned economy and, in this way, perennially inflationary pressures can play an important part in the eventual conquest of the market economy by the bureaucracy. This is because frictions and deadlocks are attributed to market failure, and used as arguments for further restrictions and regulations. A situation may arise in which a majority of people might consider central planning as the lesser of the two evils. They would be unlikely to describe such a system as socialism or communism, and exceptions would be made for small producers such as farmers and retailers.

With the advantage of more than thirty years' hindsight, it is possible to see that perhaps Schumpeter misjudged the extent to which citizens of the advanced economies would be prepared to apportion blame as between the market economy and the public-sector bureaucracy for the disappointment of their expectations. As we have seen, it does seem as if the public-sector bureaucracy may be even more unpopular than the market sector. And the 'shrinking' of the world through improvements in communications has made people aware of the failure of experiments in central planning in other countries.

In addition to the traditional remedies outlined in the foregoing paragraphs, all of which have been tried and failed, post-war governments in the United Kingdom have adopted other measures in an attempt to control inflation. They have first of all introduced legislation which attempts to diminish the influence and the bargaining power of the trade unions. It would be fair to say that the political power of the unions has so far proved too strong to permit any effective diminution of their powers. The second measure which has been adopted is to abandon the full employment goal and to allow traditional market forces to adjust the level of employment to the rate of money wage increases. Pursued in conjunction with a relatively strict monetary policy, it is argued that the objective is to lower the expectations of trade unions concerning the feasible rate of money wage increases. It is too early yet to say whether the moderation of trade union wage demands in the contemporary United Kingdom will be prolonged beyond the period of the present recession. If not, and if there should be a return to substantial wage demands well in excess of productivity increases once the present recession is over, then it is clear that whichever government is in power will impose a statutory wage and price control system, of a duration longer than any hitherto contemplated. This would be a major step in the direction of a command economy and away from a market economy. In my view, it would be a step in the wrong direction. As I have emphasized throughout the book, what is required is government action to make the market economy more flexible, rather than less flexible.

Should one trade union use its bargaining power, for example through control of the supplies of one or two key commodities, to attempt to enforce its demands, then successful resistance on the part of the government would depend on two factors. First, the political support of the population as a whole and, second, political will. One factor without the other would be ineffective: together these factors would be irresistible.

Depletion and pollution

It is too early to say anything very conclusive about the depletion of non-renewable natural resources. The problem can be divided into two parts: first of all, allowing market forces to carry the burden of adjustment; and secondly, judging the extent to which market forces, left to themselves, will incorrectly estimate the optimal rate of depletion over time. For most such resources, the rate of depletion determined by government-regulated markets will be faster than that which would be determined by unregulated markets, and the rate of depletion determined by unregulated markets is probably faster than that which is optimal. Such, however, are the uncertainties involved in the comparatively long time horizon, in the rates of discovery and in the technology of processing techniques, that the scope for variation in estimates of the optimal rates of depletion for any non-renewable resource is very wide indeed.

So far as pollution is concerned, the growth of pollution of air, water, sea and land as a result of accelerating industrial production since the Second World War has precipitated a number of specific abatement measures which have been passed through the legislatures of the advanced countries. As their name suggests, these measures do not have the objective of eliminating pollution or even of reducing it: the most they can hope for is to diminish its rate of increase. The political pressures in favour of pollution are much stronger and better organized than are those which are constituted by the environmentalist groups who, though possessed of a greater intensity of feeling, represent no powerful interests. Continuation of the present situation may reflect the predominance of a certain material gain for the present generation against an uncertain non-material loss for future generations.[2]

Discontent

The redistribution of income through taxation and the

provision of welfare benefits, which has been a characteristic feature of most of the advanced countries in the post-war period, might be thought to represent a policy against discontent. However, the discontent we are discussing in this book arises, not from a shortage, but from an abundant supply of material goods. The 1960s was the most prosperous post-war decade in the advanced countries, and yet it was also discontented. It may be that in 1968 France was bored, as it was said to have been in 1848.[3] Amongst the other discontents which we can observe as being associated with the operation of a market economy are uncertainty, alienation, inequality and the disturbance arising from the process of change itself.

Although these discontents may be softened by the introduction of an appropriate principle of social obligation, and although increased leisure and the reversal of the division of labour are also promising developments in this respect, it cannot be denied that the outlook is not bright. Technical change is likely to continue to accelerate: rationalism is likely to spread its baneful influence still wider and deeper, and the risk of extinction from nuclear processes (whether ostensibly peaceful or military) is bound to grow with the proliferation of nuclear technologies. Only the discontent which arises from excessive material consumption is avoidable, and even this depends on a marked change of attitudes on the part of the population of the advanced countries, a change which may not be forthcoming.

Extension of state control

Leaving aside the tiny minority in the advanced countries who were opposed in principle to the extension of state control, the process had gone unchallenged, indeed had accelerated, until quite recently. The reasons for the recent apparent change in public attitudes are perhaps twofold: first, governments have failed to satisfy the expectations which they have aroused, particularly concerning their performance in the field of economic policy. Secondly to the extent that the state-controlled sector grows faster than national output (and to the extent that it is not producing marketable goods), it will represent an increasing tax burden on each citizen. These tax costs are more acutely felt than the diffuse and often intangible benefits which each citizen receives from government.

Policies so far directed against state control have concentrated on the relatively simplistic objective of reducing the total numbers of state employees or, what amounts to much the same thing, total government expenditure, without any regard to the marginal costs and benefits of the particular functions affected. Although, as we have said, there is no general theory of bureaucratic behaviour, it is possible to advance a few propositions based on observation. First, it is clear that the bureaucracy as a whole will give priority to attaining their own objectives in terms of career and pensions before attending to their purported objectives. Thus, when requested to make any cuts in its expenditure, a bureaucratic organization will always put forward as a potential sacrifice that activity which affects its position the least, and which may have the highest social benefit. In this way, cut-backs in state activity generate considerable political resistance, as the public is made to feel that any cut-backs necessary involve major sacrifices in the services which they are receiving. An outstanding recent example of this was the proposal by the British Foreign Office to sacrifice large parts of the BBC's World Service broadcasting as their contribution to overall expenditure cuts. Although this broadcasting service was one of the most cost-effective parts of the whole Foreign Office budget, it was peripheral to the particular interests of the bureaucratic hierarchy and could therefore readily be sacrificed. Furthermore, the proposal had the added advantage of attracting an outcry against the principle of government expenditure in general, thus diverting attention from the question of the optimal distribution of expenditure cuts within the Foreign Office itself.

For these reasons, resistance to the reduction of state

control is very strong, indeed many might think insuperable. Despite their best intentions neither the Thatcher nor the Reagan governments have yet been able to reduce the level of public expenditure in their countries. As with other areas of policy, success in the long term will depend upon the collective will. For the collectivity, as for the individual, there is a learning process.

One of the facts which has been learned by citizens of the advanced economies in the post-war world is that governments are subject to the same limitations of imperfect knowledge and uncertain awareness of the future as are individual and corporate agents in the market economy. This experience has not been acquired costlessly, as the fate of inhabitants of high-rise housing blocks goes to show. Throughout the western world, such housing schemes have proved to be a failure for reasons never envisaged by those who designed them. The post-war expansion of the state sector has been accompanied by a degree of 'policy blindness', that is, a tendency to rush to conclusions and to action on the basis of an inadequate understanding of social and economic behaviour. In an increasingly interventionist economy, governments have to make more and more economic decisions in the light of imperfect knowledge. If the government is seen to be wrong, it thereby reduces its own legitimacy. Right or wrong, the government provides a focus of hostility for political pressure groups (for example, nuclear power-station programmes).

Today, it seems that the danger of extreme dogmatism in the field of economic policy may be past. In the eighteenth century, great cruelties were carried out in evicting crofters from their lands in the Scottish Highlands, primarily because those who carried out the evictions, as well as the leaders of the society who encouraged them to do so, acted in the conviction that what they were doing was the most progressive and scientific thing to do in the light of contemporary knowledge; and that those opposing them were ignorant and reactionary. In the twentieth century, kulaks were to suffer an even worse fate on a very much larger scale in the Soviet Union. As experience proves the limitations of government, the resistance to rolling back the boundaries of state control will start to crumble. Again, it must be emphasized that this does not constitute an argument for private ownership of the means of production. Public ownership is desirable so long as it operates within the framework of a market economy and is not protected by monopoly or other privileges.

Despite the predictions of Marx, Schumpeter and some contemporary commentators, the command economy with its associated political dictatorship appears to be an unlikely option for the advanced democracies of the present day. On the contrary, it is likely that they will make the transition to a rather different type of economic and social system. This may be described by contrasting it with its two predecessor systems.

First, there is the combination of private ownership of the means of production with the unrestrained operation of the market economy to which Marx gave the name 'capitalism'. For most of the advanced countries, this system can loosely be placed in the pre-industrial or early industrial stages of their development, that is, in the nineteenth century. It was associated with a high degree of mobility of labour, the malleability of capital and a substantial expansion of the division of labour. By modern standards technical progress was slow, but the economic system was highly flexible, and its mode of operation was tacitly accepted by the majority of the population.[4]

Since about the turn of the century the advanced economies have gradually moved into what may be described as a socialist system characterized by the accumulation of large lumps of highly specific industrial capital, a centralized technology, a lack of mobility of labour and the development of attitudes of entitlement rather than obligation. In this system, the division of labour has reached its highest point, and technical progress has accelerated, yet the market economy in most advanced countries shows signs of inflexibility in response to the resistances it has created.

We may now, in turn, look forward towards a post-industrial society, which, as its title suggests, will devote the greater part of its economic activity to the supply of services rather than industrial goods. It will further be characterized by highly sophisticated, rapidly changing, science-based technologies, which will permit, amongst other things, decentralized production. Thanks to government support for change, the economy will be more flexible than in the previous phase; the division of labour will come to a halt, and may even be reversed.

Although this economic system may be characterized by public ownership of the larger firms, and might therefore be described as a form of market socialism, it should be clearly distinguished from the mixed economy which exists in most of the advanced countries at the present time. The latter can be described as a heavily distorted and constrained market economy operating within the framework of largely private ownership. Post-industrial societies should remove many of these burdens from the market economy, while allowing societies to enjoy the rents which accrue from its more successful operations.

A summing-up

An adequate theory of the economic growth of the advanced economies is lacking. This theoretical gap has existed since at least the turn of the century, since when the nature of the advanced economies has changed markedly in many respects. Nevertheless, the ingredients for an understanding of the contemporary economies of the advanced countries are still to be found in some of the propositions of the classical political economy, upon which contemporary economic analysis has inexplicably turned its back. These propositions include, principally, the development of the market economy through the extension of the division of labour, the nature of competition in a market economy and the evolution of institutions and attitudes.

Taking each of these principles in turn, we can see that technical progress has replaced territorial expansion as the principal scope for the extension of the division of labour. However, despite the accelerating rate of technical progress in the modern world, there are reasons for believing that the extension of the division of labour may be slowing down, and may even be reversed in the near future. Despite major changes in almost all other respects, the nature of competition in the market economy remains virtually unchanged since the middle of the nineteenth century. Competition between firms takes place principally through cost-cutting and/or quality-enhancing innovations.

Over the past century, and arising directly or indirectly from the operation of the market economy, institutions and attitudes in the advanced countries have evolved which, on balance, are limiting on the effective operation of that system. These constraints include taxation, regulation and the growth of the public sector or, more precisely, the publicly owned non-market sector. A pessimistic view of the future is that these tendencies are irreversible, and will lead inevitably to advanced societies characterized by emotional enfeeblement and political dictatorship. An optimistic view is that the advanced countries, through democratic political processes, have the opportunity of influencing their future by acts of collective, as well as individual choice, and further, that they have the capability of learning from experience.

Nevertheless, it is the self-generated constraints upon the economies of the advanced countries of the present day which are primarily responsible for some of the major economic problems, such as inflation and unemployment, which beset these economies. These problems arise from an inadequate adjustment of these economies to exogenous changes, changes which are a permanent and continuous feature of a market-economy system. Thus a theory of growth of the advanced economies must be composed of two linked parts. The first part concerns the long-term development of the system, and the second part consists of medium-term adjustment to exogenous changes, the nature of the adjustment depending in part on factors created by the long-term growth of the system.

One of the universal characteristics of advanced economics has been the gradual extension of government control over economic activity, to the point where the contemporary 'mixed' economic system is quite different from the untrammelled market economy which prevailed in the nineteenth century. This phenomenon has a number of important aspects. First, there is the question of the limits of government control beyond which democracy may not survive. In this connection, it is important to bear in mind the distinction between limited and unlimited government, on the one hand, and the distinction between elected and non-elected government, on the other. Although a non-elected government, such as that of Hong Kong, may choose not to use its unlimited power to control its economic system in detail, many economists, such as Schumpeter, are sceptical that an elected government will be able, in the long run, to maintain such a self-denying ordinance.

The principal purpose of this book has been to argue that our understanding of the behaviour of the contemporary advanced economy is vitiated by the lack of a satisfactory theory of the operation of the market economy. At the same time, analysis of the behaviour of a contemporary mixed economy is incomplete, since we lack a theory of the behaviour of the public sector or, more exactly, of that part of the public sector which is not controlled by market forces.

A third aspect of the extension of government control over an advanced economy is the tendency for levels of social division, strife and discontent to be thereby increased, as each individual or group in society feels that their own material interest can best be promoted through the political process, rather than through the market.

But we have also observed how the unconstrained operation of the market economy generates its own discontents. This is scarcely surprising: we should not expect the market economy to satisfy our psychic as well as our material needs. With a diminishing urgency of needs in the advanced countries, there is scope for the re-admission of an ethic of service to the community. This would restore the balance envisaged by

Smith, which has subsequently (and understandably) swung in the direction of the pecuniary motive. The political forces which would support such a move would include the desire to solve the problem of unemployment in the advanced countries. However, a solution to this problem should not be confined to economic measures; it may be that service to the community will engender that self-respect which at the present time appears to be derived uniquely from earned income.

The present economic and social system in the advanced countries is evidently a transitional one: the present mixed economy is hardly a stable system. The successor stage will be very different from that envisaged by either Smith or Marx, but we should make use of the tools which they provided, in order not only to discern its features more clearly, but also to influence its shape and characteristics.

Notes

1 *Introduction*

1 It may be asked why the post-colonial literature of economic development has drawn so slightly on the classical tradition of economic growth. Although it is not the purpose of this book to enter into the sociology of knowledge, it may be speculated that one reason was the reluctance of Western economists to appear to be interfering in the politically sensitive area of institutional change.

2 The term 'political economy' is often used by those who are preoccupied with the theory of distribution in its aggregate form, for example, in G. C. Harcourt, 'Decline and Rise: The Revival of Classical Political Economy', *Economic Record*, vol. 51, 1975. Elsewhere, 'political economy' is sometimes used to describe studies in social economics or in economics and politics, as, for example, in the book by B. S. Frey, *Modern Political Economy*, London, 1980. A third use of the term 'political economy' by contemporary economists refers to the Keynesian policies adopted by the Kennedy administration in the United States, as represented by Walter W. Heller, in *The New Political Economy*, New York, 1965. Finally, it is sometimes applied to the economic analysis of political behaviour, for example in D. A. Kibbs and H. Fassbender (eds.), *Contemporary Political Economy*, Amsterdam, 1981.

3 J. S. Mill, *Principles of Political Economy*, London 1865, preface.

2 *Objectives of Economic Policy in the Advanced Countries*

1 The member countries of OECD are Australia, Austria, Belgium, Canada, Denmark, Finland, France, West Germany, Greece,

Iceland, Ireland, Italy, Japan, Luxemburg, the Netherlands, New Zealand, Norway, Portugal, Spain, Sweden, Switzerland, Turkey, the United Kingdom and the United States.

2 For further details, see *Economic Outlook*, Paris, July 1981.

3 A more cynical explanation is that only about 4 per cent of the *total* population (equivalent to about 10 per cent of the working population) are likely to be unemployed in an advanced economy of the present day, whereas perhaps 80 per cent of the population (all those over the age of 15) are either affected by inflation or may believe themselves to be affected by it.

4 For a detailed study of the effect of inflation on the working of financial institutions, see C. W. MacMahon, *Bank of England Quarterly Bulletin*, March 1981.

5 A. Maddison, 'Economic Policy and Performance in Europe, 1913–1970' in C. M. Cipolla (ed.), *The Fontana Economic History of Europe Volume 5: The Twentieth Century*, London 1977, chapter 9.

6 The same view is argued at greater length in P. McCracken *et al.*, *Towards Full Employment and Price Stability*, Paris, 1977.

7 These effects were identified as 'harmful tendencies' in E. J. Mishan's first book, *The Costs of Economic Growth*, London, 1967, but by the time of his second book, *The Economic Growth Debate*, London, 1977, they had become 'irreversible trends'. This argument is disputed by W. Beckerman in *In Defence of Economic Growth*, London, 1974.

8 Mishan, *The Economic Growth Debate*, p. 10.

9 E. J. Mishan, *Welfare Economics: An Assessment*, Amsterdam, 1969, p. 78.

10 Government intervention may be measured in a number of ways. Marxists would presumably measure the degree of intervention by the proportion of productive assets which were state-owned, and Keynesians, apparently, by the proportion of a country's gross domestic product accounted for by government expenditure. Following Schumpeter, I believe that it is the extent of control exercised by a government in a market economy which is decisive.

11 See J. A. Schumpeter, *Capitalism, Socialism and Democracy*, 3rd edn, London, 1949.

3 *The Failure of Contemporary Economic Analysis*

1 By analysis, I mean both theory and the application of theory.

My argument is not that economic analysis has failed to solve the actual economic problems of the modern world, but that it has failed to offer an adequate understanding of contemporary reality.

2   Critics include T. C. Koopmans, *Three Essays on the State of Economic Science*, New York, 1957; A. Lowe, *On Economic Knowledge*, New York, 1965; M. M. Postan, 'A Plague of Economists', *Encounter*, January 1968; W. W. Leontief, 'Theoretical Observations and Non-Observed Facts', *American Economic Review*, March 1970; E. H. Phelps Brown, 'The Underdevelopment of Economics', *Economic Journal*, March 1972, D. O'Brien, 'Whither Economics?', *Economics*, Summer 1975; H. Katouzian, *Ideology and Method in Economics*, London, 1980. Defenders are represented by J. R. N. Stone, 'Political Economy, Economics and Beyond', *Economic Journal*, December 1980.

3   A. T. Peacock, 'From Political Economy to Economic Science', *University of Edinburgh Journal*, vol. 18, no. 4, 1957.

4   D. J. Smyth and J. C. K. Ash, 'Forecasting GNP, the Rate of Inflation, and the Balance of Trade', *Economic Journal*, June 1975.

5   Stone, 'Political Economy, Economics and Beyond', p. 733.

6   Lowe, *On Economic Knowledge*, p. 3.

7   O'Brien, 'Whither Economics?' p. 23. The same author quotes Boulding's illustration of his generalized Heisenberg principle: a patient, asked about his health, replies that he is fine, and the effort kills him.

8   H. G. Johnson, 'The Economic Approach to Social Questions', *Economica*, vol. 35, 1968, pp. 1–12.

9   The crude quantitative-methods approach has been satirized many times, most recently in H. Katouzian, *Ideology and Method in Economics*, London, 1980, chapter 8. Unfortunately, this has not so far had a sufficiently deterrent effect.

10   H. G. Johnson, 'A Catarrh of Economists', *Encounter*, May 1968, p. 53.

11   M. Abramowitz, 'The Theory of Economic Growth', in H. S. Ellis (ed.), *A Survey of Contemporary Economics*, Homewood, Illinois, 1952.

12   F. H. Hahn and R. C. O. Matthews, 'The Theory of Economic Growth: A Survey' in *American Economic Association Surveys of Economic Theory*, vol. 2, New York, 1965.

13   D. Bell and I. Kristol (eds.), *The Crisis in Economic Theory*, New York, 1981, p. 218.

14   W. W. Rostow, 'Comment from a Not Quite Empty Box', *Economic Journal*, March 1982, p. 160.

4   *The Classical Tradition in Growth Theory*

1   To avoid repetition, the word 'neo-classical' will henceforward be used to include 'Keynesian'.

2   Although recent interpretations of Smith's work have focused attention on his theory of distribution (see, for example, P. A. Samuelson, 'The Canonical Classical Model of Political Economy', *Journal of Economic Literature*, December 1978), Myint has convincingly demonstrated that the principal welfare objective of classical economics is to attain a continuous state of economic expansion, rather than to tighten up the equilibrium allocation of resources (see H. Myint, *Theories of Welfare Economics*, London, 1948, p. 87). Indeed, it is precisely the continuous growth of output which acts as a balancing mechanism in both the labour-market and the capital market in Smith's theory of economic growth. Myint goes so far as to argue that Smith would advocate interference with the given time preference of savers in order to expand the total volume of economic activity: 'to Adam Smith and his followers it was evident that the dynamic gain from expanding economic activity would be so great and widespread as to swamp all waste from interfering with the static allocative equilibrium' (p. 60).

3   J. S. Mill, *Principles of Political Economy*, London, 1865, p. 13.

4   A. Smith, *The Wealth of Nations* (1776), New York, 1937, book V, chapter 1, p. 706.

5   The view that Ricardo represents a detour in the classical tradition is supported by J. A. Schumpeter in his *History of Economic Analysis*, Oxford, 1954.

6   E. Streissler, in J. R. Hicks and W. Weber (eds.), *Carl Menger and the Austrian School of Economics*, London, 1973, p. 165.

7   Apart from Smith himself, this school of thought included Robertson, Millar, Hume, Kames, Dunbar and Adam Ferguson. The influence of these writers upon later classical economists, notably Marx, is traced in the article by A. S. Skinner, 'Economics and History: the Scottish Enlightenment', *Scottish Journal of Political Economy*, February 1965.

8   Aristotle, *Politics*, Book 1, 1252A.

9   Note that this foreshadows the Austrian view of the process of economic growth.

10   Adam Smith, cited by Skinner, 'Economics and History', p. 9.

11   'Without private property there would be no industry, and without

industry men would remain savages for ever' (Kames, *Sketches*, Dublin, 1775, vol. 1 p. 70).

12   Adam Smith, cited by Skinner, 'Economics and History', p. 13.

13   Skinner, ibid., p. 17.

14   I. Adelman, *Theories of Economic Development*, New York, 1964, p. 41.

15   A. Smith, *Wealth of Nations*, book 4, chapter 9.

16   Cf. the 'growth theory' attributed to Smith by J. R. Hicks in *Capital and Growth*, Oxford, 1965, chapter 4.

17   A. Lowe, *On Economic Knowledge*, New York, 1965, p. 169.

18   A. Smith, *The Theory of Moral Sentiments* (1759), London, 1880, pp. 263–4.

19   The importance which capital accumulation played in Smith's theory of economic development may be seen from the following passage: 'every increase or diminution of capital . . . naturally tends to increase or diminish the real quantity of industry, the number of productive hands, and consequently the exchangeable value of the annual produce of the land and labour of the country, the real welath and revenue of all its inhabitants' (Smith, *Wealth of Nations*, book I, chapter 3, p. 321).

20   Ibid., book V, chapter 1, part 2, p. 670.

21   S. Hollander, *The Economics of Adam Smith*, London, 1973, p. 266.

22   The distinction between 'socialism' and 'communism' is hardly sufficiently large to justify considering these as two stages rather than one.

23   A. Gray, *The Development of Economic Doctrine*, London, 1933, p. 309. Marx's view of human nature has been interpreted more sympathetically as follows: 'the distinctive character of man's humanity for Marx lies in his ability to engage in consciously planned action, directed towards the realisation of his ends' (M. Howard and J. King, *The Political Economy of Marx*, London, 1975, p. 2).

24   C. Menger, *Problems of Economics and Sociology* (1883), Urbana, Ill., 1960, p. 93.

25   Menger, ibid., p. 172.

26   F. A. Hayek, *The Counter Revolution of Science*, London, 1955, p. 83.

27   K. Popper, *The Poverty of Historicism*, New York, 1964, p. 65.

28   Hayek, *The Counter Revolution of Science*, p. 80.

29   F. A. Hayek, *The Road to Serfdom*, London, 1944.

30   But see S. C. Littlechild, *The Fallacy of the Mixed Economy*,
     London, 1978, p. 14.
31   Cited in D. Seckler, *Thorstein Veblen and the Institutionalists*,
     London, 1975, p. 67.
32   J. A. Schumpeter, *Capitalism, Socialism and Democracy*, London,
     1949, p. 141.
33   See P. Berger, *Modernisation and Religion*, Dublin, 1981, for the
     view that modernization does not necessarily imply secularization.
34   Schumpeter, *Capitalism, Socialism and Democracy*, Preface.

5   Division of Labour and the Process of Change

1   K. Marx, *Manifesto of the Communist Party* (1888), New York,
    1955, p. 13.
2   G. L. S. Shackle, *The Nature of Economic Thought*, Cambridge,
    1966.
3   A. Smith, *Wealth of Nations*, (1776), New York, 1937, p. lvii.
4   A. Young, 'Increasing Returns and Economic Progress', *Economic
    Journal*, December 1928, p. 529.
5   L. Von Mises, *The Ultimate Foundations of Economic Science*,
    Kansas, 1962, p. 126.
6   Young, 'Increasing Returns and Economic Progress', p. 536.
    Young's interpretation is disputed by Myint. Myint asserts that
    capital accumulation was regarded by Smith as being an even
    more important determinant of the division of labour than the
    widening of the market. According to this view, even if the market
    were not widened but capital accumulation were increased, this
    would increase the demand for labour and call forth an increased
    population which, in turn, would offer scope for increases in
    productivity. Thus, Myint says, Smith thought that increases in
    population alone would increase the productivity of labour. Cf.
    H. Myint, *Theories of Welfare Economics*, London, 1948, p. 5.
7   Smith, *Wealth of Nations*, p. 706.
8   It is interesting to observe that elsewhere Marx evolved a quite
    different theory of growth which is closely related to the modern
    steady-state growth theory of the neo-classical variety. This
    theory, or theories, consists of two-sector steady-state models
    which Marx calls simple and expanded reproduction schemes.
    They are frequently quoted by Marxists (extensively by Brody),
    but seldom is any attempt made to reconcile these theories with
    Marx's classical analysis of the growth process in the market

economy. Sherman, however, claims that Marx's steady-state models refer to the socialist stage of development, but this explanation appears to be contradicted by the terminology which is used by Marx in the description of his models. Amongst other anomalies, these models observe Say's Law. See H. Sherman, *Radical Political Economy*, New York, 1972, pp. 378–86.

9   Both Schumpeter and other Austrians agree that a piece of new information will disrupt some agent's existing plan and cause him to revise it. Schumpeter labels this as 'disruptive' of equilibrium, whereas other Austrians regard it as a movement towards equilibrium. The differences seem to be only semantic.

10 The essence of the 'profit incentive' is thus not to be seen as a motivation to work harder or to allocate resources more efficiently. The profit incentive operates more significantly by sparking the alertness of entrepreneurs — by encouraging them to keep their eyes open for new information that will lead to new plans.

11 J. M. Clark, *Competition as a Dynamic Process*, Washington, 1961; and also, 'Toward a Concept of Workable Competition', *American Economic Review*, June 1940.

6   *What has happened in the Advanced Economies*

1   J. A. Schumpeter, 'The Instability of Capitalism', *Economic Journal*, vol. 38, pp. 361–86. The passage just quoted shows that Schumpeter's essential idea was formulated fourteen years before it was elaborated in his book, *Capitalism, Socialism and Democracy*, New York, 1942. An assessment of the accuracy of Schumpeter's prediction is contained in the volume edited by A. Heertje, *Schumpeter's Vision*, New York, 1981.

2   The empirical evidence concerning the increasing concentration of firms is inconclusive.

3   Amongst the major commercial risks facing firms in the contemporary advanced countries are those created by the uncertainty surrounding future rates of inflation and taxation. Neither was a major factor in the nineteenth century. Today no corporation, however large, could afford the risk of issuing an index-linked bond.

4   M. Particelli, *Outlook* no. 4, London, 1981.

5   'What improved and still improves the fecundity of human efforts is the progressive accumulation of capital goods without which no technological innovation could be practically utilised. No tech-

nological computation or calculation would be possible in an environment that did not employ a generally used medium of exchange, money . . . The quantification of physics and chemistry would be useless for technological planning, and I might add, for economic planning (if there were no economic calculation). What is lacking to the under developed nations is not knowledge but capital' L. Von Mises, *The Ultimate Foundations of Economic Science*, Kansas, 1962, p. 127.

6   For example, at the present time in many of the advanced countries, socialist parties are protesting about the 'de-industrialization' of the economy.

7   E. J. Mishan, *Welfare Economics, An Assessment*, Amsterdam, 1969, p. 78. Although it may be argued that this criticism applies to all forms of industrial society, irrespective of the method of resource allocation, it is the market form which has prevailed in all the advanced countries.

8   See Kenneth Boulding, 'Economics as a Moral Science', *American Economic Review*, March 1969.

7   *The Origins of some Contemporary Problems*

1   S. Nora, *The Computerisation of Society*, Cambridge, Mass., 1980.

2   In an unpublished paper, the late J. P. Mackintosh wrote of this phenomenon: 'the whole social, political and industrial atmosphere in Britain leads managers to believe, correctly, that they will lose any confrontation'.

3   This is not to deny that in particular periods in particular countries the prevailing level of unemployment might have been reduced by an increase in the aggregate level of monetary demand. It is to deny that differences *between* countries, and over longish periods of time since the war *within* countries, can be explained by deficiencies in aggregate monetary demand.

4   Such tasks need not be (though they often are) particularly dirty or dangerous, domestic service being an example.

5   The fact that the nastier jobs are often the lower-paid supports the notion of non-competing groups in labour-markets. This, in turn, undermines the nineteenth-century liberal position of treating all men equally. Unswerving attachment to this belief seems to have cost the Liberal Party the support of the working class in the UK in the early twentieth century, though it has not perceptibly damaged so far the Democratic Party in the US.

6   These impressions may be substantiated by recent statistics of unemployment by occupation in Scotland, compared to vacancies:

Occupational class	*Ratio of unemployment/vacancies*	
	June 1980	*June 1981*
Managerial and professional	4.9	8.2
General labourers	71.0	126.3

Source: Department of Employment, 1980 and 1981.

7   It is not clear whether the work ethic means the feeling that work is good as an end in itself or because it is a contribution to society or because it enhances self-respect. Does it enhance self-respect solely because it is a contribution to society?

8   The origins of the ideal view of physical labour have been expressed as follows: 'immediately next in order after consent to suffer death, consent to the law which makes work indispensable for conserving life represents the most perfect act of obedience which it is given to Man to accomplish. It follows that all other human activities, command over men, technical planning, art, science, philosophy and so on, are all inferior to physical labour in spiritual significance. It is not difficult to define the place that physical labour should occupy in a well ordered social life. It should be its spiritual core.' (S. Weil, *The Need for Roots*, London, 1949, p. 287).

9   The populations of the two major countries who lost the war (Germany and Japan), perhaps chastened by defeat, entertained more realistic expectations and appeared more willing to accept the traditional disciplines required for the successful operation of the market economy.

10   Schumpeter's 1949 diagnosis of the problems of the UK economy still holds true more than thirty years later. Two passages are worth quoting: 'the basic difficulty is excess consumption, that is, a real wage bill plus the real cost of social services which are, on the one hand, incompatible with the other conditions for the English economy at its present level of productivity and, on the other hand, obstacles which prevent it from rising to a higher level'.

     He foresees that 'the fundamental condition for durable success is adjustment of the economic process in such a way as to make it once more produce, along with the goods for her domestic consumption and the goods and services that are to pay for her imports, a genuine net surplus for investment at home and abroad. This cannot be accomplished without a temporary decrease of consumption and permanent increase in production; and these in turn cannot be brought about without an unpopular reduction in public expenditure and a still more unpopular shift in the burden of taxation. On weighing the implications of this, the reader will have no difficulty in realising the magnitude of the political problem involved. Whatever has to be achieved will be achieved by difficult manoeuvring at an indefinite number of points. It seems reasonable to expect that nowhere will success go beyond the absolute minimum because, things being what they are, every move will bear interpretation as an uncompensated sacrifice of some vested interest of labour.' (J.A. Schumpeter, *Capitalism, Socialism and Democracy*, London, 1949, preface to the third English edition.)

11   See, for example, D. H. Meadows, *The Limits to Growth*, New York, 1972.

12   J. Peterson and C. Fisher, 'The Exploitation of Extractive Resources', *Economic Journal*, December 1977.

13   W. W. Leontief, *The Future of the World Economy*, New York, 1977.

14   Royal Commission on Environmental Pollution, Sixth Report, *Nuclear Power and the Environment* (Chairman Sir Brian Flowers), Cmnd 6618, London, 1976.

15   E. J. Mishan, *Welfare Economics: An Assessment*, Amsterdam, 1969, p. 78.

16   It might not be too fanciful to suggest that the huge growth in domestic public-sector employment in the post-war UK provided employment opportunities to compensate for the loss of similar opportunities in the overseas Empire, the administration of which was once described as a system of outdoor relief for the middle classes. As we have seen, the alternative of opportunities in business seemed less attractive as the capitalist ethos was on the wane.

17   There is the related point that the extension of government responsibility into a wider range of human activity can lead to increased social conflict and tension. This is analogous to the idea that fruit can be obtained by shaking trees.

18   An illustration of this proposition is provided by the university system in the United Kingdom. Since the war, British universities have been financed largely by direct grants from the government.

For this reason, they have been unable to respond to changing demands in higher education, notably for adult education and distance learning methods.

8 *Prospects for the Future of the Advanced Economies*

1   J. A. Schumpeter, *Capitalism, Socialism and Democracy*, London, 1949, preface to third English edition.
2   Although it is true that this government came to power shortly before the second major post-war round of oil price increases, it is also true that the UK, alone amongst the industrialized countries, is more than self-sufficient in crude oil.
3   This inactivity may, in large part, be explained by the unfortunate experience of its predecessors. The Wilson government's proposals for trade union reform contained in the White Paper *In Place of Strife* had to be withdrawn as a result of pressure from the unions, and the Heath government's Industrial Relations Act eventually proved to be unenforceable.
4   F. A. Hayek, *The Road to Serfdom*, London, 1944, p. 79.
5   Ibid., p 84.
6   In a recent essay, Professor Gottfried Haberler compares pairs of countries alike in most respects, including their material living standards, prior to the establishment of a socialist regime in one member of each pair. Haberler suggests that their subsequent relative economic development constitutes significant empirical evidence of the inferior performance of the socialist system compared even to 'fettered capitalism'. His pairs of countries are West and East Germany, Austria and Czechoslovakia, Greece and Yugoslavia, Thailand and Burma, China and Taiwan, Puerto Rico and Cuba. See A. Heertje (ed.), *Schumpeter's Vision*, New York, 1981, chapter 4

9 *A Note on Method*

1   Hayek has two things to say about differences between the natural sciences and the social sciences which are germane. 'We [economists] do not know as sharp a division between the theoretician and the practitioner as there exists between the physicist and the engineer or between the physiologist and the doctor. This is not

an accident or merely an earlier stage of development but a necessary consequence of the nature of our subject. It is due to the fact that the task of recognising the presence in the real world of the conditions corresponding to the various assumptions of our theoretical scheme is often more difficult than theory itself, an art which only those acquire to whom the theoretical schemes have become second nature . . . We can therefore only rarely delegate the application of our knowledge but must be our own practitioners, doctors as well as physiologists.'

'The degree of abstraction which the theoretical disciplines in our field requires makes them at least as theoretical, if not more so, than any in the natural sciences. This, however, is precisely the source of our difficulty. Not only is the individual concrete instance much more important to us than it is in the natural sciences, but the way from the theoretical construction to the explanation of the particular is also much longer.' (F.A. Hayek, *Studies in Philosophy, Politics and Economics*, London, 1967, p. 464, 469–70.)

2   Practitioners of quantitative methods in economics have frequently overlooked some of the basic theoretical propositions in the subject, such as that price is a determinant of quantities supplied and demanded.

3   I. M. T. Stewart, *Reasoning and Method in Economics*, London, 1979, p. 182.

4   F. A. Hayek, 'The Dilemma of Specialisation', in L. D. White (ed.), *The State of the Social Sciences*, Chicago, 1956, p. 463.

5   H. Katouzian, *Ideology and Method in Economics*, London, 1980, p. 182.

6   Ibid.

7   E. H. Phelps Brown, 'The Underdevelopment of Economics', *Economic Journal*, March 1972, p. 10.

8   W. Leontief, in A. Brody, *Prices, Proportions and Planning*, Budapest, 1970, p. 7. This, of course, is just as true of the natural sciences as it is of the social sciences.

9   D. A. Reisman, *Adam Smith's Sociological Economics*, London, 1976, p. 45.

10 It is therefore all the more strange that Marshall should have attempted to do this.

11 J. A. Schumpeter, *Capitalism, Socialism and Democracy*, London, 1949, pp. 416–17.

12 See, for example, G. C. Harcourt, 'Decline and Rise: The Revival of Classical Political Economy', *Economic Record*, vol. 51, 1975.

13   A good example of the impression of settled truth which is falsely
      conveyed in contemporary teaching concerns the Phillips curve.
      Students are taught that the coincidence of unemployment and
      inflation may be explained by the outward shifting of the Phillips
      curve. As Katouzian points out, 'this argument is little more than
      a tautology: we have no evidence that "the curve has been shifting",
      and the expected rate of inflation is almost impossible to know.
      Yet we assume that this unknown expected rate has been different
      from the actual, so we leave the curve no choice but to shift . . .
      This so-called explanation increases the socio-economic stock of
      "natural" concepts by one more; namely, the empirically indeter-
      minate concept of the "natural" rate of unemployment: this is the
      rate of unemployment at which that unknown and perhaps un-
      knowable expected rate of inflation equals the actual rate. Thus,
      almost any rate of unemployment would conceivably qualify for
      being "unnatural".' See Katouzian, *Ideology and Method in Econ-
      omics*, p. 17.
14   Shortly before these words were written 364 British economists
      attached their names to a statement on economic policy which
      was given wide circulation and considerable publicity in the press.
      One does not have to disagree with the contents of the statement
      to say that it made no contribution whatsoever to any policy
      debate. Economists have only themselves to blame that they have
      voluntarily excluded themselves from discussions of major policy
      issues by the too narrow interpretations which they have placed
      on their subject. Nor should raising the level of public debate be
      regarded as a modest objective: it is surely the highest objective
      which an economist, acting in his public-policy role, could hope
      to achieve.
15   Hayek, *Studies in Philosophy, Politics and Economics*, p. 288.

10   *Conclusions*

1   The following passage draws heavily on Schumpeter's farewell
      address to the American Economic Association, published as
      J. A. Schumpeter, 'The March into Socialism', *American Economic
      Association Papers and Proceedings*, May 1950.
2   But as one US Senator is alleged to have observed: 'what did
      posterity ever do for us?' It is interesting to contrast this inter-
      temporal chauvinism with the traditional hostility evinced by

conservatives towards the alleged intergenerational burden of the national debt.

3   F. Guizot, *Mémoires*, Paris, 1870.
4   'Of all the struggles for emancipation none commands such universal assent as does the Promethean revolt of modern technology against Adam's Curse' (A. Lowe, *On Economic Knowledge*, New York, 1965, p. 13).

Index